Alexander the Fabulous

Alexander the Fabulous

*The Man Who Brought
the World to Its Knees*

Michael Alvear and Vicky A. Shecter

Advocate
BOOKS

Manufactured in the United States of America.

This trade paperback original is published by Advocate Books,
    an imprint of Alyson Publications,
P.O. Box 4371, Los Angeles, California 90078-4371.
Distribution in the United Kingdom by Turnaround Publisher
    Services Ltd.,
Unit 3, Olympia Trading Estate, Coburg Road, Wood Green,
London N22 6TZ England.

First edition: November 2004

04 05 06 07 08 ✳ 10 9 8 7 6 5 4 3 2 1

ISBN 1-55583-897-9

Library of Congress Cataloging-in-Publication Data
  Alvear, Michael.
    Alexander the fabulous : the man who brought the world to
  its knees / Michael Alvear and Vicky Shecter.
    Includes index.
    ISBN 1-55583-897-9 (paper)
    1. Alexander, the Great, 356–323 b.c.—Sexual behavior.
  2. Greece—History—Macedonian Expansion, 359–323 b.c.
  3. Generals—Greece—Biography. 4. Greece—Kings and rulers—
  Biography. I. Shecter, Vicky. II. Title.
  DF234.2.A44 2004
  938'.07'092—DC22   2004057078
  [B]

Credits
Cover illustration by Jeehe Lee.
Cover design by Matt Sams.

*To everyone who sees lightning
and thinks it's God snapping their picture.*

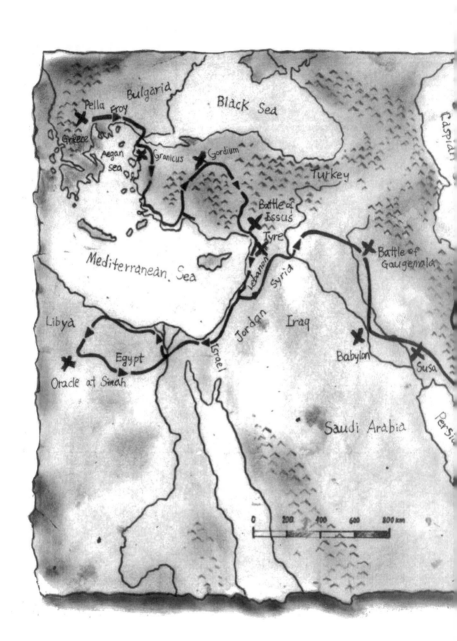

Contents

Acknowledgments

We'd like to thank Alexander the Great for making our job so easy. We couldn't have made up this shit if we'd tried. He is without question one of the most important figures in history. He's certainly one of the most entertaining.

We'd also like to thank a certain ten-year-old member of our family who perfectly captured our obsession with Alexander. We were working in his mother's office, which was littered with dozens of books, maps, and images of Alexander. When we asked him what he thought of the mess, he replied, "Alexander is Mommy's new boyfriend." We were going to say, "Actually, Uncle Michael would probably have a better crack at him." But he'd already run out of the room. That's the problem with kids today: They never sit still long enough to let the grown-ups get a good jab in.

We'd also like to thank the man who made the book possible: Marc Acito, who referred us to Alyson.

Last, we'd like to thank our editor, Nick Street. He wisely cut the lame jokes and gleefully accepted the unusual comedic devices we proposed. But mostly we thank him for letting us offend as many people and cultures as possible.

Timeline

(Before the Common Era)

Philip and Olympias have hot monkey sex on the set of *My Big Fat Greek Orgy*. They marry later that year.

356 BCE

Alexander is born. Comes out of womb complaining about the harsh lighting.

346 BCE

Alexander, 11, tames his legendary horse Bucephalus (Greek for "Frankencock").

343 BCE

Aristotle tutors Alexander for the next three years. 14-year-old Alexander meets Hephaestion, whom he describes as "pure shagability."

340 BCE

Philip appoints 16-year-old Alexander regent of Macedonia. Alexander is pissed. Wanted to be "reigning queen" not "acting king," but Olympias objected. Enraged, Alexander leads Macedonian army to victory over the Thracians.

338 BCE

Alexander and Philip defeat Thebes. The rest of Greece pees in its collective loincloth, proclaims Philip King of unified Greece.

337 BCE

Philip falls in love with Eurydice, threatening Alexander's ascension and Olympias' status as mother to Philip's successor. She and Alexander, 19, exile themselves to nearby Epirus and declare Philip "nothing but chewed up club trash."

336 BCE

Philip killed. Alexander, 20, ascends the throne, tries out the tiara. Olympias does Snoopy's "Dinner Dance."

335 BCE

Alexander maintains his title as King of all Greece by ending the revolt at Thebes. Actually, he ends Thebes altogether. Takes on barbaric tribes to the north, crosses the Danube, fortifies northern frontiers, defeats the Illyrians, and memorizes the lyrics to the musical *CATS*.

334 BCE

Alexander, 22, penetrates Persia. Not a snug fit. Finally gets traction, winning Battle of Granicus. Claims western end of Turkey for Greece.

333 BCE

Alexander, 23, solves riddle of Gordian Knot, wins first Persian conflict—the Battle of Issus—conquering all of Turkey. Goes online with sassy screen name ("Fuknhotblond") and provocative profile ("strong stick, velvet throat"), trades pictures and meets the beautiful eunuch Bagoas at a Starbucks.

332 BCE

Alexander wins his most gruesome battle—the siege of Tyrus (they spilled cauldrons of red-hot sand on Alexander's men). Also takes territories in Libya, Lebanon, and Syria. Crowned Pharaoh in Egypt, Evita in Argentina, and Barbra in Los Angeles.

331 BCE

Oracle at Siwah confirms Alexander's belief that he is "simply divine." Now 25 years old, he establishes Alexandria in Egypt. Wins Battle of Gaugamela (Iran), and defeats King Darius, thereby claiming all of Iraq and Iran. Persia officially becomes Alexander's bitch.

330 BCE

Eyebrow waxing at Persian spa goes horribly awry. A vengeful Alexander torches the fabled city of Persepolis (in present-day Iran).

328 BCE

Alexander, 28, murders Black Cleitus in a drunken brawl. When a despondent Alexander threatens suicide, a philosopher asks him, "Would Zeus second-guess himself?" Problem solved.

327 BCE

Alexander captures Sogdian Rock in Afghanistan, but Osama Bin Laden still manages to slip away. Alexander invades Roxane and marries India.

Wait! Reverse that.

326 BCE

Alexander defeats King Porus in Battle of Hydaspes, winning part of India (today's Pakistan). Beloved horse Bucephalus dies. Separate sarcophagus needed for horse's genitals. Alexander's men revolt. Want a change of underwear and a one-way ticket home, thwarting Alexander's plans for conquering rest of India. On the way back to Greece, Alexander, 30, takes an arrow to his lung and narrowly averts death. Recovers when trusted generals blast Gloria Gaynor's "I Will Survive."

325 BCE

Thousands of Alexander's men die on the terrible march through the Gedrosian Desert. Some from thirst, most from heartbreak (the sand ruined their Manolo Blahniks).

324 BCE

To achieve his vision of a "raceless" world, Alexander, 32, orders mass weddings at Susa (in present-day Iran) between his Macedonian men and Persian women. Alexander marries two Persian women to cement the link between the two cultures. And triple his wardrobe.

Hephaestion dies. Alexander is devastated; never truly recovers from his grief. *New York Times* obituary lists Hephaestion as Alexander's "longtime companion."

323 BCE

Alexander, 33, dies in Babylon (modern Iraq) after 10 days of illness. The hardest part of the funeral preparations: prying the mirror out of his hand.

322 to 321 BCE

All hell breaks loose. Power struggles between generals. Murder. Mayhem. Shopping. The Greek Empire fractures into four territories.

320 to 30 BCE

Hellenism flourishes for almost 300 years. Greek traditions and practices permeate the known world, profoundly influencing religion, politics, architecture, and web design.

30 CE (Common Era)

Cleopatra dies, taking with her the last remnants of Hellenism (she was related to Alexander). Rome becomes the empire du jour, with the promise of fresh pasta in every pot.

49 BCE to 476 CE

Rome rules the world, making punctuality a cultural relic and ass-pinching a part of every school curriculum.

350 CE to 1400 CE

Christianity becomes the official religion of the Roman Empire, heralding the Empire's collapse and ensuring the destruction of every spark of human creativity and expression for centuries. Sometimes known as the Ashcroft Era, more commonly referred to as the Dark Ages.

1100 CE

Christians lead "the Crusades," plundering the Arab world to wrest control of Jerusalem from the heathens. Discover that Arabs preserved the works of Aristotle and other Hellenistic geniuses. Word leaks out and the West "re-discovers" Alexander, romanticizing him in the book *Boys Gone Wild, Doggie Style.* Also known as *The Romance of Alexander.*

14th to 16th Centuries

Aristotle's works and the stories of Alexander's conquests are translated from the Greek to Latin, capturing the imagination of the West. The educated class becomes fascinated by the classical Greek world, beginning an era of astounding artistic and scientific creativity—the Renaissance.

1946

Sikander, the first movie about Alexander, produced in India, of all places. Scene 3 has Aristotle warning Alexander that his love for women is distracting him from conquering the world. Actor playing Aristotle wins Academy Award for saying the line without bursting into laughter.

1956

Alexander the Great is the first American movie about the hero, starring Richard Burton. Proves Burton can't act unless he's holding a bottle of scotch or Elizabeth Taylor's breasts.

2004

Oliver Stone releases his own film about Alexander the Great. Claims Alexander was assassinated by a conspiracy involving Fidel Castro, the Mafia, and the CIA.

Introduction

"When Alexander saw the breadth of his
domain, he wept for there were no
more worlds to conquer."
—Plutarch

For the one and only time in history, a single man ruled the
planet. Alexander the Great was quite literally king of the world.
He conquered most of the lands known to the Greeks, unified
them with a common language, imbued his empire with religious
tolerance, and enriched it with racial diversity. He founded close
to 70 cities across Turkey, Asia, Central Europe, and the Middle
East. He created new trade routes and replaced barter and
exchange economies with a single monetary system. He ushered
in a cultural, scientific, and economic renaissance that persisted
for almost 250 years after his death and still affects us today.

Not bad for a homo.

This man who was in love with another man influenced just
about every major religion in existence today, including Islam,
Judaism, Buddhism, and Hinduism. Historians also credit him

with something that should give fundamentalist Christians a stroke: Alexander the Homo established the cultural milieu that set the stage for the birth of Christianity.

Alexander is most famous for his mojo as a military man. His armies marched a total of 22,000 miles *on foot* to conquer the known world. He is without question one of the greatest military heroes who ever lived. He was brilliant, audacious, and savage. And even though he was wounded by every conceivable weapon, he never lost a single battle.

So much for the standard hetero history lesson. Let's get to the interesting part.

Alexander was *hot,* his boyfriends were hotter, he threw hissy fits that would take Liza Minnelli's breath away, he had

fag hags hanging off him like laundry, and he loved the arts (especially music and theater). It's the interplay between his personal fabulousness and his public greatness that makes Alexander the Great one of the most exhilarating characters in world history.

Alexander hadn't intended to remake the world. He merely wanted to be the greatest hero of all time—greater than Achilles or Heracles (a.k.a. Hercules). But even Alexander wasn't immune to the law of unintended consequences. As you'll read in this book, Alexander was responsible for many aspects of life we take for granted, like raves and circuit parties and that thing you never use: your gym membership.

The most disappointing thing about researching this book was realizing the degree to which historians have ignored or deliberately misrepresented Alexander's sexuality. As if acknowledging his attraction to men would somehow diminish his accomplishments. Or, worse, as if he accomplished all that he did *despite* his attraction to men. Scholars, especially the earlier ones, describe Alexander's 19-year love affair with his boyfriend Hephaestion as a "close friendship." The more edgy scholars describe it as an "exceptionally close friendship." Never mind that scrolls from antiquity attest to Alexander's romantic love for Hephaestion. The most direct—and hilarious—reference comes from the Cynic philosophers, who lived about 2,000 years ago. They wrote: "Alexander was only defeated once, and that was by Hephaestion's thighs."

When it comes to giving context to their subject's achievements, many scholars apply a double standard to the importance of a hero's romantic life. If he loves women, it's essential. If he loves men, it's irrelevant. Would any thoughtful scholar describe Julius Caesar's love affair with Cleopatra as a "close friendship?"

That concludes the soapbox portion of the book.

Well, OK, one more thing. We can't continue without noting a certain irony: History's greatest military leader could not serve in today's armed forces. This despite the fact that Grant, Patton, MacArthur, and Schwarzkopf *combined* didn't come close to achieving what Alexander did. And if you locked all five warriors in a room and threw in a knife, only Alexander would walk out without needing medical attention. And he'd walk out like Evita too: On the balcony, arms outstretched, greeting the adoring crowds below.

Different historians have different interpretations of Alexander's character and achievements. For instance, modern historians think he was an alcoholic. Ancient historians thought he hardly touched the stuff. After poring through dozens of books and historical Web sites, we came up with a strategy for reconciling the sometimes staggeringly different perceptions of Alexander. For the most part, we stuck with mainstream consensus thinking and focused primarily, of course, on the thinking that offered the most comic opportunity.

All dates, people, places, and sexual positions were carefully researched. This book takes potshots at the truth, but it's not a work of fiction. We're proud to say we've lampooned Alexander's life without sacrificing historical accuracy.

So get ready to meet Alexander the Fabulous—the man who went down on history and came up smiling.

Chapter 1

Coming From Crazy

If Alexander exhaled drama it's because that's all there was to breathe in his house. If the writers of *The Young and the Restless, Days of our Lives,* and George W. Bush's preemptive strike policies got together, they couldn't have come up with the kind of plutonium-grade dramatics that pervaded Alexander's home. He was born to an alpha-bastard father and a beta-bitch mother. They loathed each other with the kind of intensity runners-up feel for the winners of beauty contests.

Historians say Alexander's father, Philip, was a notorious philanderer, which meant he'd stick it in anything with a pulse. As the king of Macedonia, his royal scepter had rights to all the thighs in the land. And he exercised those rights left and right, up and down (and a little to the side). He did it all, of course, in view of his wife, Olympias Dukakis, who played Cher's mom in *Moonstruck.* Olympias started life as Princess Polyxena Myrtale, and was later renamed "Olympias" because her royal family supposedly descended from one of the 12 Olympian gods.

At the time, Greece wasn't a country the way the United States is a country. They had no fast food, strip malls, Game

Boys, or tractor pulls. There wasn't so much a "Greece" as there was a collection of cities loosely related by language and religion but not politically bound to each other. So cities like Athens, Sparta, Macedonia, and Corinth were called "city-states." Imagine Los Angeles and San Francisco but no California or America and you get the picture.

The more sophisticated city-states, like Athens, considered Macedonians the rednecks of antiquity—people who lit up cigarettes when they farted and blew the wheels right off their mobile homes.

Philip was king of the Mediterranean rednecks. Like many conservatives today, he had a certain fondness for weapons. If Charlton Heston hadn't beaten him for the presidency of the National Rifle Association, it would have been Philip who'd have thrilled the NRA crowd by

proclaiming, "I have only five words for you: from my cold, dead hands."

Philip ascended the throne the old-fashioned way—by killing anybody who got in his way. He got the nod when his brother King Perdiccas (pronounced "You sure got a purdy ass") died in battle.

When King Philip took over, Macedonia was still a backwater intellectual and cultural hellhole. When he was done, Macedonia was a well-armed backwater intellectual and cultural hellhole.

Militaristic Neanderthal that he was, Philip truly did revolutionize warfare and lay the groundwork for Alexander's later successes. First, though Sparta created the first "professional army," Philip took that institution to a new level. Most armies during antiquity were just ragtag, come-as-you-are, somebody's-trying-to-kill-us affairs that disbanded as soon as the threat was over. Philip was the first Macedonian ruler to make military service a professional occupation that paid well enough to attract soldiers who would enlist for years at a time.

Second, Philip invented one of the most powerful weapons of the time: the sarissa. It was an 18-foot wooden pike with a metal tip. When any number of sarissas were held upright by rear-row infantrymen, they helped hide maneuvers from view of the enemy. When held horizontally by front-row warriors, they were rather brutal weapons. The ability to impale people 20 feet away was a huge advantage when wars were basically hand-to-hand combat.

Third, Philip perfected the military "phalanx," which is Latin for "fear of size queens" (*Phallus Anxietus*). It was also a specific battle line formation made up of highly disciplined battalions that marched in lockstep. Doesn't sound very original except that, until then, wars were basically a helter-skelter, every-man-for-himself swarm against the opponents.

Philip was a brilliant military general in the ancient world—on par with Julius Caesar—but his place in history is eclipsed by the fruit of his loins: Alexander.

And speaking of springing, here's how Alexander sprang: Philip, ever on the lookout for new tail, sailed to Samothrace, where the local religion involved fertility rituals that featured binge drinking, throbbing music, and hubba-hubba hug-a-hunk-and-get-drunk dancing. Sound familiar? Yes, the White Party started in Greece, and it moved to Palm Springs 2,000 years later.

It was at the drink-drenched party-with-a-purpose that

Philip fell in love with Olympias. She was his third wife. What happened to the first two? Nothing. He was still married to them. To Philip, monogamy was a board game by Milton Bradley.

Olympias was the daughter of the king of Epirus, so the marriage gave Philip powerful political ties. Nobody knows for sure what Olympias looked like, but she was said to be beautiful. One story has it that 200 soldiers of an invading army were sent to kill her in her home, but they took one look at her face and decided they couldn't do it. In fact, they were so moved by her beauty they backed up into each other, which gave the Greeks a few other ideas.

Alexander got his legendary looks from both of his parents. In his youth, Philip was described as handsome, but he eventually acquired so many battle scars his face looked like a connect-the-dots game. When Philip got his eye gouged out in battle many people thought the damage improved his looks.

But what Philip didn't have in looks he made up for in personality. He's credited with originating the irritated customer's classic put-down for chatty service people: "How would you like your hair cut, sir?" a royal barber once asked. "In silence," Philip replied.

Olympias' family was said to have descended from Achilles. This "fact" of her lineage set the stage for the mythology of greatness that would later surround Alexander. Yes, his mother thought her son was a god. To support this belief, Olympias claimed that Alexander was conceived when a thunderbolt hit her G-spot and spread a fire from her womb to the ends of the earth. Who says kegeling doesn't pay off?

So in the month of August, 356 years before Christ was born, Alexander burst out of his beautiful but delusional mother under the sign of Leo, the lion. *Roar.*

Alexander's primary early relationship was with his mom. Daddy was off fighting (and winning) wars all the time.

Like all women of the era, Olympias was "given" in marriage. She had no say and no rights, so she couldn't do much about Philip's philandering. Not that she cared. She was more interested in making Alexander the heir apparent than keeping her husband faithful. She was turned on by power, not fidelity.

Olympias wasn't the type of woman who just dipped into the cooking sherry every now and then. The woman could *drink*. She was a devotee of the Mysteries, a sect that honored Dionysus, the god of wine, orgiastic abandon, and ecstasy (the mood, not the pill). As part of her devotional life, she favored mystic rituals and loved torchlit fertility rites.

Olympias was also an expert at handling snakes, which scared the bejesus out of even seasoned warriors. According to Plutarch, Olympias would conceal the snakes under her gown and make them rear their heads to terrify Philip and his men. Once Philip spied on Olympias through a crack in their bedroom door and saw a huge snake slithering around her body. He freaked out—he thought a god had come to earth in the form of a snake to make love to her or, worse, that she wasn't planning to invite him to the party.

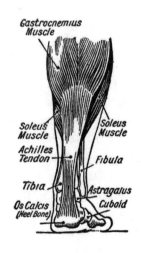

Olympias never missed an opportunity to remind people that she was descended from Achilles, the legendary warrior of Homer's *Iliad*. The gods made Achilles impossible to kill by dipping him in magic waters at his birth. The magic waters, however, didn't cover his heels, where he was gripped during his dunk.

Achilles' enemy, Paris of Troy (the pretty boy who kidnapped Helen and started a ten-year war), figured out Achilles' weakness and shot poison arrows into his heels. Contrary to popular belief, the phrase "Achilles' heel" has nothing to do with Manolo Blahnik's new warrior pumps; it refers to a person's fatal weakness. This is an important story (Achilles, not the pumps), because Alexander would later model himself after Achilles.

After Paris kidnapped Helen from Sparta, the Greeks were outraged. The most beautiful woman in Greece was "stolen" from them. When they unleashed their navy on Troy, Helen became known as the "face that launched a thousand ships." As opposed to Philip, who became known as the face that could make a pug wince.

In addition to his hetero activities, Philip also had a retinue of homosexual lovers. (Did the man ever sleep?) Men weren't just undoing his pants: they were eventually his undoing. Philip was, in the end, killed by a jilted male lover named Pausanias, whom Philip had replaced with a younger man. This did not sit well with Pausanias, who got drunk at a party and called his replacement a paid whore. The replacement whore wanted to disprove the aspersion cast on his honor, so he ran ahead of the fighting line during a border war into certain death at the hands of the enemy.

A friend of Philip's (some think it was the replacement whore's family or tribal chief) decided to exact revenge on Pausanias by getting the original whore drunk as a skunk and throwing him to the horny slaves, who ravaged him.

Pausanias went to Philip (newly bowlegged, presumably) to demand vengeance. Ordinarily, Philip would have simply executed the man who threw Pausanias to the slaves, but, unfortunately for Pausanias, the man had lots of powerful political connections. Philip ended up giving Pausanias money and a higher rank as recompense for his humiliation. The limping Pausanias was not happy. Indeed, he would eventually get his revenge by killing Philip himself.

The one thing that united Philip and Olympias was their love for young Alexander, who was said to be precocious, even brilliant. They imported prestigious teachers from all over—including the teacher of all teachers, Aristotle—to meet the boy's insatiable intellectual curiosity. While the rest of the Macedonian kids were listening to Hooked on Phonics, Alexander was learning at the foot of one of the great masters.

By the time Alexander was a teenager his parents were bitter enemies. He had one sister, Cleopatra (no, not the Cleopatra played by Elizabeth Taylor—Cleopatra was a pretty common name back then), who was born not long after him. Part of the problem between Philip and Olympias was the king's polygamy. She didn't really give a care where he dipped the royal wick, and she didn't really care that he took four additional wives *while they were married.* What she cared about was remaining queen. And the only way to do that was to be the mother of the anointed heir.

It was said that Philip took a new wife with every war. This, of course, left Olympias more shaken than a martini. With more wives came more children. And more children meant more competition for Alexander's spot. It became increasingly likely that Olympias would lose her role as queen. As long as Philip's other wives were politically unimportant and bore only girls, Olympias left them alone. Still, she constantly gave her rivals the Leona Helmsley death glare.

Olympias always had a problem with anyone who came between her and Alexander—whether it was his father, his lieutenants, or his lovers. She once sent Hephaestion, Alexander's boyfriend, an angry note in which she complained about Hephaestion's meddling. Hephaestion wrote back, "Stop quarreling with me: Not that in any case I shall much care. You know Alexander means more to me than anyone."

When Alex was 18, his parents began to worry about his "sexual interests." It wasn't that they feared he might become an activist and land on the cover of *The Advocate* under the headline, WE'RE HERE, WE'RE QUEER, WE'RE TAKING OVER KASHMIR! On the contrary, man-on-man love was of no consequence to the Greeks, and certainly not to Philip, who took whatever and whomever he could get.

Alexander's parents were merely concerned about his producing an heir for the next generation. For his part, Alexander was not thrilled with the concept. Some historians say he was appalled by the idea of marriage, especially given the raging, spiteful nature of his parents' union. His reluctance to marry probably also has something to do with the fact that, by the time Alexander was 18, hunky Hephaestion had already been heating up Alexander's sheets for years.

Olympias continually nagged Alexander about marrying and is said to have hired a famous *hetaira* to "het" him up. Hetairas were rich, beautiful, and educated (a rarity among women in Greece at the time). They were often accomplished musicians and artists. But a hooker's a hooker, even if she can quote Plato and play a lyre.

Yes, Olympias hired a prostitute for her son! One can only imagine Alexander's reaction to the gift: "Gee, Mom, thanks. You shouldn't have."

It's clear that Alexander's sexual appetite wasn't nearly so ravenous as his father's. Apart from Hephaestion and the Persian boy toy Bagoas, ancient historians have little to say about Alexander's sex life. Apparently, the world's greatest conqueror was also one of its greatest romantics.

Philip was quite proud of Alexander's precocity. When Alexander was 16, Philip named him regent to Macedonia (acting king). Philip was busy putting out fires throughout the lands he had conquered and needed someone to watch the fort. Alexander didn't just watch the fort; he expanded it. His first test as regent was the rebellion of the Maedi, a gang of barbaric villagers who hung out in the hinterlands plotting attacks against the Macedonians. Alexander kicked ass, took over and consolidated their territories, and renamed the region Alexandropolis. This was the first of many cities Alexander would name after himself. (Vain? The boy-king makes Donald Trump look positively shy.)

During the battle for Thrace, a nearby city-state, Philip and Alexander had a major falling-out. (Keep in mind, the two men often fought side by side on the battlefield—their version of father-son bonding.) Alexander claimed he saved his Philip's life when a riot broke out between Macedonian soldiers and Greek mercenaries and Philip, caught unawares, fell down and pretended to be dead. To hear Alexander tell it, he used his shield to protect Philip while he fought and defeated men with his own hands. Alexander felt that his father was too ashamed to admit his son saved his life. Philip claimed that Alexander exaggerated the story to puff up his reputation. There is no corroboration on either side, but clearly the two men had different interpretations of events. Still, when they were at war and away from Olympias, father and son usually got along famously.

When Alexander turned 18, he and Philip were on good terms. Then Philip ruined the rosy glow by falling in love again. But not just with anybody. He fell in love with a girl from noble Macedonian stock. If she gave birth to a boy, there would be plenty of people who would say, "Dump the crazy snake-handling witch from Epirus and her girlie-man son." On top of that, the Macedonian princess was only 15—three years younger than Alexander, who couldn't believe his father would endanger his right to the throne.

Once again, Alexander was stuck in the middle of a raging fight between his parents. Alexander reportedly said to Philip, "When my mother remarries I'll invite *you* to *her* wedding." Wives couldn't have multiple husbands, so by saying this Alexander was not only defending his mom but developing into one of the first feminists in history. (He would later treat women with uncommon dignity and respect.)

The question remained: Would he attend Philip's latest wedding and hurt his mother's feelings or skip the nuptuals and insult his father? In the end, he chose to attend the wedding feast, but only to keep tabs on what was going on. And much drama ensued.

Philip's good friend Attalus—an uncle of the bride—made a toast at the wedding feast. In it, he said he hoped the union between Philip and his new *pregnant* bride would produce a "legitimate heir" for Macedonia.

You might as well have told a drag queen her shoes didn't match her purse. Alexander's talons sprang out and he shouted, "What about me, you blackguard? A bastard am I?"

Then, like Liza Minnelli caught by photographers without her makeup on, Alexander hurled his goblet at Attalus' head. Attalus launched his own goblet at Alexander. In the melee, Alexander said something to his father (no one knows what), which prompted Philip to draw his sword and lurched menacingly toward him. Would the king kill his son? Would Alexander be a gay Oedipus, killing his father and sleeping with his mother's boyfriends?

In the end, the party guests were spattered with no one's blood. Philip, drunk and hobbled by war injuries, did a faceplant on the floor before he could reach the mignon he wanted to filet.

"Look men," Alexander reportedly said with a laugh. "He's getting ready to cross from Europe to Asia, and he falls crossing from couch to couch."

Before Philip could sober up and finish what he'd apparently started, Alexander hightailed it to mama and told her to pack her bags. Off they went over the rugged mountains to the dominion of Olympias' brother, who had succeeded her father as the king of Epirus.

Alexander and his mother were humiliated. By allowing Attalus to question Alexander's legitimacy as heir apparent, Philip had brought to life Alexander's worst nightmare: competition for the throne. Olympias had plenty of reason to be anxious too: If the son of one of Philip's other wives was anointed heir to the throne, she would last about as long as a virgin at a barbarian convention.

Philip and Alexander began to reconcile within a few months, primarily because Alexander helpfully conquered some bothersome tribes. Nothing softened Philip's heart more readily than a son who kicked land and grabbed ass. Or was it the other way around?

Alexander finally kissed and made up with his father when Philip's new wife had a baby girl, thus removing a potential challenge to Alexander's claim to the crown. Meanwhile, the brazen battle-ax, exiled in Epirus, was so full of rage toward Philip that she talked her kingly brother into declaring war against Macedonia. Philip managed to avert war by offering in marriage to his brother-in-law a most tempting bride: Alexander's sister, Cleopatra! You'd think Olympias' brother might have said, "But she's my niece!" Instead he replied, "Where do I sign?"

Alexander and Philip had made peace but they were still wary of each other. Philip was jealous of Alexander's ability to forge friendships with men who would die for him or pledge to protect him at any cost. In Philip's eyes that kind of loyalty was potentially treasonous. It was for the king that men should give their lives, not the king's son.

In the meantime, during this uneasy truce between father and son, rumors abounded that Philip was going to arrange a marriage between Arrhidaeus, Alexander's retarded half brother (from Philip's first marriage), and a daughter of a powerful ruler in Asia Minor (present-day Turkey). This arrangement would either make Arrhidaeus or the son he might bear ripe for succession.

There was no way Alexander was going to let his half-wit brother take the throne away from him, so he hatched a plot. He asked his friend Thettalus, a leading tragic actor, to impersonate one of Philip's secret emissaries and pay a visit to the ruler in Asia Minor. Philip's "emissary" called Alexander's half brother a "fool and bastard" and offered Alexander's hand in marriage instead. The leader—being no fool himself—jumped at this offer. Everyone but Alexander was confident that Alexander would be Philip's successor.

When Philip discovered their plot, all hell broke loose. It wasn't just Alexander's running around behind his back that ticked him off. He was appalled by the idiocy of Alexander's marrying a woman who would do little for the empire: The woman did not come from a dynasty powerful enough to support Philip's vision for Macedonia.

Philip went berserk. He broke off the wedding engagement and placed Alexander under house arrest. He also banished all of Alexander's close friends except for Hephaestion, whom Philip considered a good influence on his son. Philip admired that Hephaestion had continued to exchange letters with Aristotle for years after the philosopher left Macedonia. Philip also knew that their "special" relationship made Hephaestion a useful hostage should the need arise. The king was nothing if not practical.

Why couldn't Alexander see what was obvious to everyone else? Philip would never choose anyone but him to be successor. He had proved himself as a warrior and diplomat. Besides, everything he heard about Philip's plan to arrange a marriage for Arrhidaeus turned out to be nothing more than unsubstantiated rumor. Historians aren't certain who spread the rumors, but they're pretty sure her initials were O.L.Y.M.P.I.A.S.

Speaking of Witch, Olympias was spitting nails at the attention the new bride was getting. Philip gave her the name of his mother, Eurydice, a sign that a new queen was emerging. All Eurydice had to do was whelp a boy pup and it was all over for Olympias—the exit door was about to hit her on the ass. Two years after their marriage, that's exactly what Philip's teenage bride did.

Sure enough, Philip decided to divorce Olympias. Actually, there was no divorce back then. Hell, he had seven wives! Philip simply declared Olympias would no longer be queen. She was no stranger to being stripped—but not of her title. In Olympias' mind this meant a fight to the death, and she had no plans to die young.

Meanwhile, Philip had succeeded in uniting all of Greece. He planned to use the united Greek front to knock Asia Minor back into the previous century and steal all their gold. To celebrate his big plans he invited all the delegates of the Greek city-states to a nonstop rave party of banquets, public games, and musical performances.

On the second day of the festival, Philip was to walk into the amphitheater to launch the Olympian games (where events like the javelin throw were performed naked, which was always a sure-fire crowd-pleaser). Instead of being flanked by his bodyguards, Philip decided to show the world he was just a "regular guy" and walked into the arena alone. No homeys, no peeps, no posses.

Now, there are two ways to a man's heart—through the chest with a sharp knife or with a category-five blow job. Unfortunately, Philip did not get head that day. By walking into the arena unattended he gave his killer a clear shot with a sharp blade. Philip sank to his knees, clutched his heart, and fell face-first at the feet of the honored guests.

Meanwhile, the killer made a mad dash for the exit when he tripped over a vine—the idiot—and was savagely hacked to bits by Philip's men. Recall who killed Philip? Pausanias, the former lover Philip had dumped for a younger boy. The circle of betrayal was complete. Cue the music, fade to black, cut to commercials.

Once everyone realized Philip had been killed, all the chiefs and nobles crowded around Alexander, forming a ring of protection (nobody was armed since this was a sacred ceremony). There was no question in anyone's mind: Alexander was the new king of Macedon. The year was 336 BCE. Alexander was 20 years old.

Most historians think Olympias was the mastermind behind the murder. After all, Philip's demise came soon after Eurydice's baby boy was born. Many historians believe that Olympias incited Pausanias' lingering anger to get him to do the dirty deed.

After the murder, what was left of Pausanias' corpse was nailed to the gallows in a public courtyard. That night Olympias placed a gold crown on his head (a mark of glorification). Later, she burned the murderer's body over Philip's ashes and buried them in a nearby grave. Until her death, she gave thanks over Pausanias' grave every year on the anniversary of Philip's murder. She also had the murder weapon dedicated to Apollo. Olympias made Joan Crawford look like Joan of Arcadia.

While her husband's ashes were still warm, Olympias went after Eurydice and her children. Some say she strangled the newborn boy in front of his mother, who then, in her grief, hung herself and her baby girl. Others say Olympias tied her former rival to a brazier (picture an ancient barbeque spit, otherwise known as an altar fire) and roasted her alive.

Some historians believe Alexander helped his mother plan the murder. Their detractors believe he was not morally capable of it. The gods cursed parricide, and Alexander, who was devoutly religious, would never have crossed them.

But what if Alexander didn't believe Philip was his father? Since he was a child, Olympias had been stuffing Alexander's head with the story that she had actually mated with Zeus to conceive him. Back then, people sincerely believed that gods mated with humans. Many people still do. Belief in the Virgin Mary's Immaculate Conception isn't so far removed from this aspect of Greek mythology.

Though Aristotle, a scientists' scientist, could find no proof of gods procreating with humans, he never publicly questioned the idea. Public outrage at his blasphemy would have compelled him to drink hemlock.

Even so, it's highly doubtful that Alexander would have conspired to kill Philip. Philip and Alexander had been planning to go to war, which was always a wonderfully bloody father-son bonding affair. If he'd really wanted to kill Philip, it would have made more sense to do the deed in the heat of battle, where his actions could have been easily hidden in the fog of war.

When Alexander left Greece to conquer the world not long after Philip's death, he said goodbye to his mother at the palace, not realizing that he would never see her again. For almost 13 years he would march through Persia (present-day Iran), Egypt, India, and Pakistan, claiming them all for his empire.

He left his general Antipater as regent of Greece while he campaigned. Olympias hated Antipater, probably because she couldn't rule him like she wanted. She wrote long, complaining letters to her son, the new king. After one of her particularly heated rants against Antipater, Alexander, exasperated, turned to Hephaestion and is reported to have blurted out something along the lines of: "She's charging pretty high rent for the nine months' lodging she gave me."

Yet the bond between Alexander and Olympias was too great to be broken by her constant complaining. She regularly sent offerings and dedications to the gods on Alexander's behalf, and he, knowing how devout she was, was certain the gods heard her. When Antipater wrote to complain about Olympias, Alexander reportedly said, "One tear shed by my mother would wipe out ten thousand letters such as this." He answered Olympias' letters faithfully and sent her lavish gifts from the lands he plundered.

Years later, when Alexander died, Olympias became a marked woman. She was no longer queen, which meant she no longer had protection from the families of the people she had screwed over and killed. At first she survived by running back to Epirus to be with her daughter. But the hatred she had sowed in the hearts of her enemies eventually caught up with her. Some say she was executed by the man who eventually took over Macedon—Antipater's son, no less. Others say she was lynched. Still others say the army couldn't bring itself to execute the mother of the man they idolized, so they delivered her to the people who could—the families of those she had murdered. And that was the end of the mother of all mother complexes.

Chapter 2

Mirror, Mirror, on the Wall, Who's the Prettiest Conqueror of Them All?

Alexander the Great was one of the vainest men in human history. And that's the opinion of the historians who liked him.

From childhood on, Alexander was obsessed with how he appeared to people. Plutarch says he "valued his good name more than his life or his crown" and that "his passionate desire for fame implanted in him a pride and grandeur of vision which went far beyond his years."

Arrian, one of the most authoritative ancient historians of Alexander's life, says, "He was fearfully mastered by love of fame." A more contemporary biographer, Mary Renault, explains Alexander's "unpleasant concern for his own glory" as simply part of the time he lived in. Greeks believed in the Homeric ideal of excellence, which they called arête.

Arête was the dominant value in Greek life for hundreds of years. It's the ideal that suffuses Homer's epic poems the *Odyssey* and the *Iliad*. Arête was used to describe widely different traits. The arête of a racehorse was speed, of a cart horse, strength, of a porn star, girth. You achieved arête as a soldier in war and as an athlete in peace. You were considered excellent if you were skilled either at killing men in battle or beating them on the playing field. The concept of arête survives to this day. That's why seeking honor, fame, and the right table at the hottest restaurant are still considered worthy endeavors.

Socrates, Plato, and Aristotle all believed that noble Greek men should brag about their accomplishments. That's because arête was a public ideal requiring public displays. How would people know what to emulate if it were kept a secret?

It's important to understand the Greeks didn't encourage ordinary bling-bling, chest-beating, hip-hop, brag-'n'-rag pissing contests. The thing the Greeks hated most, other than ugly men with small penises, was a boastful liar. You had to have the goods to back up the brag. And by the goods they weren't talking about an ability to create stop-you-in-your-tracks window displays at Neiman Marcus. They were talking about excellence on the battlefield, in academics, in athletics, in politics. Modesty was not a prized virtue in the Greek world. You were supposed to seek praise. The catch was what you were supposed to be praised for: winning deadly fights, triumphing over enemies, withstanding physical torture.

Alexander believed himself to be the greatest among men in part because that's what he yearned to be. He quite literally believed in the creed: Fake it till you make it. He aspired to be something greater than those around him and realized early in his life that the best way to achieve his goal would be to model himself after the gods and demigods he admired. "How can a man become a god?" was a question Alexander once asked several Indian philosophers (after sacking their country, of course). They answered, "By doing something man cannot do." This pretty much sums up Alexander's attempts at missions others thought impossible. The classic chicken-or-the-egg question comes to mind: Was Alexander a god because he could do incredible things, or did doing incredible things make him a god? Even he wasn't sure. It was a question that would dominate his life.

From the beginning, Alexander's beauty and affability made him a genuinely loved child. He had gray eyes and curly hair, and it was said that a pleasant scent came from his skin and that there was a sweet fragrance to his breath. Even his sweat smelled clean. Gay, gay, *gay*!

Because many people commented on his pleasant smell, some historians surmise that Alexander must have been in exceptionally good health (sweet breath meant his teeth and digestive system were in good shape). Other scholars attribute Alexander's fragrance to coffee enemas, chelation therapy, and the Atkins diet. But they teach in community colleges, so nobody believes them.

Of Alexander's beauty there was no doubt. But vain? The man refused hot showers because they fogged the mirrors. That didn't stop him from keeping himself squeaky-clean, though. History's greatest military hero loved taking girlie baths. For a man living in an age just this side of the Neanderthals, taking bubble baths was, to say the least, highly unusual.

The only time Alexander didn't take baths was on the battlefield. "What's that smell?" he must have said, sniffing his armpits as he slit an enemy's throat. "I smell like the business end of a donkey!"

Alexander also liked to shave his chest and legs. No, wait, that was Greg Louganis. Alexander liked to shave his face. This too shocked his countrymen. Remember, the last of the Cro-Magnon men had croaked, like, three weeks earlier. If the Greeks had been born just a few generations sooner they wouldn't have been able to walk upright without dragging their knuckles on the ground.

Alexander rationalized his shaving as a combat advantage. If the enemy couldn't grab you by the beard he'd have a harder time killing you. Historians have waved their bullshit detector over that one; the results are inconclusive. Let's just say there's a whole school of thought that says Alexander didn't like hair on his face for the same reason Narcissus didn't like ripples in the water: It got in the way of his admiring himself.

Upon seeing him clean-shaven, lots of people raised their eyebrows, but nobody raised a stink. You just didn't question the guy who kicked the world's ass. In fact, Alexander started a craze and soon *everyone* was barebacking. No, that's not right. They were already doing that. Soon *everyone* was going bare-faced.

Philip must have been spinning in his grave seeing the army's energy wasted on something as girlie as shaving. "What are we running, a spa?" he would have bellowed. "What's next, botox and chemical peels?"

Alexander also believed in the perfect body. Not many people know this, but he posed for the first few covers of *Men's Health*. He valued a certain kind of body, though: an idealized image of maleness where everything was in proportion. He was a fitness buff, hitting the gym five days a week (legs Tuesdays and Thursdays, arms on Wednesdays, chest and back on Fridays and Mondays). He loved cardio too—running, hunting, and ball games. Oddly, for a world-class athlete, he hated professional athletics. He thought athletes had become too specialized and their bodies weren't "balanced" in the classical definition of beauty.

The nice thing about Alexander's ego was that it rarely got in the way of his friendships, his sense of fair play, or his belief in the virtue of sacrifice (at least in the beginning, anyway). At 12 he was the fastest runner in Macedon. "Why don't you run in the Olympics?" his friends asked. He refused. "Not unless I have kings to run against," he declared. Some say he worried that he might be "given" a race because he was the future king of Macedon. Historians differ on their interpretation of this: Either he was afraid of losing and protected his vanity by refusing to compete, or he genuinely believed it was wrong to put other athletes in the awkward position of showing up a future king. Whatever the case, his contemporaries saw his refusal to race as a sign of exceptional integrity.

Alexander had always been ambitious. Though he respected and admired his great military hero father, he was also jealous of him. While "Is it in yet?" may be the four most damaging words other men can hear, "Philip already did that" were the four most damaging words to Alexander's ego. When he was in his early teens he worried that Philip would leave him nothing to conquer. He is said to have complained, "My father will forestall me in everything until there will be nothing great left to do in the entire world!"

Alexander never did anything in a small way. Even his vanity was turbocharged. Ordinary vanity says, "I'm beautiful." Alexander-brand vanity says, "I'm a god."

If Alexander was to prove himself part-god, he had to do the miraculous. You can hardly convince someone you're a demigod if you just sit around reading back issues of *Vanity Fair*. Major victories against impossible odds were in order. Alexander felt he was Destiny's Child, but Beyoncé sued, so he had to back down from the claim. Still, he believed that fate had big plans for him.

There's a reason nobody called him Alexander the Above Average, and it wasn't just because they'd have been beheaded. They called him "the Great" because he managed to convince the world that he was, like the star of the early John Waters films, Divine.

Remember, from an early age his mother hinted that Zeus, not Philip, was Alexander's true father. In fact, Alexander often called Philip, "My so-called father." Alexander suspected he was a descendant of the gods and spent his whole life trying to

prove it to himself and others. Today if you believed you were God it would land you a talk radio show or a cot at Betty Ford, but back then it would've put you squarely in the mainstream.

What we now think of as absurd mythological stories the Greeks revered as gospel. What's fantasy to us was real to them. Example: Seers told the god Cronos, ruler of the universe, that his own son would dethrone him. Cronos avoided this fate by swallowing his children at birth. Now, two questions pop into the modern mind. First, would Pepcid AC work after a meal like that? Second, how could people believe that shit? But they did. What we know as myths the ancient Greeks accepted as fact. For instance, everyone "knew" that Apollo was the sun god and that the sun was actually the chariot he used to cross the sky every day.

Or take the story of Prometheus. He was the god who created man out of mud, and he loved his creation more than he loved the other gods. So when Zeus ordered all men to gift a portion of their kill to the gods, Prometheus tricked him into choosing the wrong gift bag. One had bones wrapped in juicy fat while the other had the good meat hidden inside. Zeus picked the pile of fat and, boy, was he pissed. His decisions became the law of the cosmos, so he couldn't take back his choice. Now the gods were stuck with fat on a bed of bones for all eternity.

To get back at Prometheus, Zeus took fire away from man. But Prometheus stuck a stick in the sun and brought fire back to us mortals. Zeus, enraged, inflicted a terrible punishment on both man and Prometheus. To punish man, Zeus had another god create a woman of stunning beauty but with a deceptive heart and a lying tongue: Jennifer Lopez. Actually, it was the first woman: Pandora. Every man wanted to be the first to open her box. She did it herself, thank you very much, and life was never the same. See, she was forbidden to open the box (a jar, really). When she did, out flew every conceivable evil, sorrow, plague, and misfortune that could be visited on the world, proving once again that behind every man stands a woman who caused all the problems.

Next, Zeus had his servants, Force and Violence, seize Prometheus, take him to the Caucasus Mountains, and tie him to a rock with unbreakable chains. Talk about being grounded with no TV privileges. Prometheus was tormented at night by a giant eagle that swooped in to rip out and eat his liver. The god's liver would regenerate during the day and attract the hungry eagle again every night.

Zeus always believed that going too far was never far enough. He did, however, give Prometheus several ways out of this torment. One of them was that a mortal must kill the eagle and unchain Prometheus. And indeed, somebody eventually killed the eagle and freed Prometheus. The mortal who rescued him? None other than one of the heroes Alexander patterned himself after: Heracles .

Like we've said, these weren't imaginary to the Greeks; they weren't fables or allegories; they were the truth. And woe to the person who questioned the truth. Imagine telling a convention of fundamentalist Christians that Jesus' resurrection was a fairy

tale. They'd give you the same limp the Greeks would have given you for questioning *their* beliefs.

Nothing was ever done in Greek life without consulting the gods. You were either favored or cursed by them, depending on your actions. The gods were churlish, petulant, jealous, and petty. They were said to live on Mt. Olympus, but their pure bitchiness leads many historians to believe they actually lived on Fire Island.

Divining what the divinities wanted and figuring out how to please them (and how to avoid offending them) was an elaborate process that entailed sacrifices, rituals, and mystical prophecies. Early on, Olympias trained Alexander to appease the gods and to follow signs and omens. He learned his lessons well. Alexander did not make a move without the counsel of seers, oracles, priests, and the occasional media consultant. He always looked for signs and obeyed them with a discipline most gay men reserve for their beauty regimens.

And if he couldn't "see" a sign from the gods, he'd make one up. Take, for example, his run-in with the oracle at Delphi when he was just 22 years old. On the way to invade Persia, he took a special detour to Delphi to ask the oracle if he'd be successful. The journey took him longer than he anticipated, and by the time he reached Delphi it was late November. Problem: The oracle didn't augur the future from November to February. Alexander had missed the foretelling "season."

During this hiatus the oracle was not to be disturbed as a matter of religious law. Not even for the king of unified Greece would the priests make an exception. Still, Alexander was famous for not taking no for an answer. Actually, he was famous for killing people who uttered that hideous word.

Ignoring the rules, Alexander sent a peremptory challenge to Pythias (basically, the head of development at Delphi Pictures; also the oracle's bouncer), demanding to see the oracle. The answer? "Talk to the hand." Well, maybe not those *exact* words. But Pythias refused Alexander's request, pointing out that it was the gods themselves who decreed that the oracle (a wild-haired crone) was not to speak again until February. Besides, Alexander's battle armor wasn't hip enough.

Alexander stormed in, seized the oracle by her hair, and literally dragged her into the shrine. "Young man," gasped the priestess, "you are invincible!" Now, the oracle had likely meant her outburst as an insult, like calling Alexander an insufferable brat who can't take no for an answer. But that's not how Alexander interpreted her words. Only someone with a planet-size ego could take a heated insult as a clear prophecy. He promptly released her and announced to his men that the gods had pronounced him *aniketos*: invincible against the Persians. It was now safe to go a-butchering.

Alexander claimed he looked to the gods for guidance, but he wasn't looking for signs. He was looking for validation. Sometimes an exceptional ass-kicking worked just as well. There was often no quicker way to get people to validate your lofty stature than by slaughtering everybody who dared suggest otherwise.

Months before his encounter with the oracle, Alexander faced his first real test as a new king. After Philip's death, many of the Greek city-states decided they had never liked the idea of a unified kingdom under a bully king, so they staged uprisings. It was their way of testing Alexander's mettle and strength. After all, at 21 he was but a young pup still wet behind the ears.

Well, said pup lay siege to the city of Thebes, butchered every-body who got in his way, and took the rest as slaves. Afterward, there *was* no city of Thebes; Alexander ordered it burned to the ground. The message he sent to Athens, Sparta, and the rest: "Don't fuck with me, fellas. This ain't my first time at the rodeo." After witnessing what he did to Thebes, Athens and the other city-states quickly said, "Just kidding...no, really, Alexander, we love you." Did somebody say "love"? Alexander loved being loved. When the city-states pledged their devotion to him, he practically purred.

Around the same time, Alexander had a very interesting con-versation with the Celts—a tribe that eventually settled an island that became known as England. The Celts came to pay tribute to Alexander after he crossed the Danube with a huge battalion. No one had ever crossed the river with so many men, and the Celts wanted to kiss Alexander's butt to discourage him from kicking theirs. Alexander crossed the river because he wanted to send a message: "We can cross this river to get you, so you better not think about crossing it to get us."

Alexander, always on the lookout for a compliment, asked them what they feared the most. He was hoping to hear "You, of course!" But the Celts were proud people. They were also very tall; in fact, they towered over Alexander. To defuse the situation, they poked fun at their height. "The only thing we're afraid of," they said, "is the sky falling on our heads." Alexander laughed ever so politely, but he was miffed. He wanted to hear, "You're our greatest fear because you're the best warrior who ever lived, you handsome thing!" He sent them away with a vow of friend-ship but not without muttering angrily, "What braggarts these Celts are!"

As things heated up in Persia, it's easy to understand why Alexander's ego was inflating faster than the turkey float in the

Macy's Thanksgiving Day Parade. At only 23 he was the king of all of Greece and had defeated the Persian army in the first of three face-offs. Beyond that, he commanded the largest army the Greeks had ever amassed. He had almost 43,000 men under him (the power-top show-off), and that was just the infantry (archers, phalanx fighters, sword swallowers, etc.). He also had almost 7,000 men in the cavalry, the elite mounted guard. As he marched through Persia he took soldiers from cities and tribes he conquered, swelling the ranks of his already formidable army, which at times numbered close to 100,000 men.

Alexander also traveled with about 1,200 engineers and laborers. These were the men who built bridges and engines of war, including catapults, battering rams, and high ladders. He needed blacksmiths to repair swords and breastplates; artisans to make and repair shoes, clothing, bows, and arrows; and people to cook food, carry water, and set up camp. He also needed people to maintain the stocks of food, which often included poaching from neighboring farms in whatever countryside they were in.

Having 7,000 men in the cavalry meant that 7,000 horses had to be taken care of and fed in addition to the 10,000 pack animals (mules, oxen) necessary for the carrying of heavy siege engines, food, water, and whatever else was too heavy for humans to carry.

Alexander was managing the logistics of tens of thousands of men and animals. It's estimated that he needed 511,000 pounds food and 1.5 million pounds of water each day. The man did not believe in traveling with a suitcase and two carry-ons. And these numbers don't reflect the slaves and concubines (and the children of slaves and concubines) the men "acquired" after each victory. To get a sense of the scale we're talking about, picture this: Alexander was marauding the world with a virtual city at his back. He was basically attacking cities with a city of his own.

The enormity of his campaigns had no equal (and still don't). The logistical and managerial nightmare posed a daunting question: How do you keep that many warriors happy and willing to conquer other lands? The answer: loot, loot, and more loot. Alexander had the god thing down; he just needed to put an *L* in there and he had the perfect spoil to keep everyone motivated: gold. Persia had tons of it, and Alexander aimed to acquire all of it in order to pay his men. Making your men believe you're a god is only half the battle when you want to keep the rank and file ranking and filing and not mutinying and revolting. The other half is payola.

The burden of maintaining such a huge entourage posed an alarming question for Alexander: Could he take Persia before the relentless warring and dwindling pay overwhelmed the morale of his soldiers? What Alexander needed was a sign, a voice from heaven, a nod from the gods.

The rituals for divining the future were strange. Imagine making the decision to invade another country based on whether a pigeon's ass twitched to the left when it took a dump. It wasn't quite that bad, but almost. Take, for example, the famous story of the Gordian Knot. It involved leather, mesh, thongs, and swordplay. And that was way before anyone created the International Male catalog. It all happened in a Turkish town called Gordium, near a temple of Zeus. There was an ancient oxcart with an odd feature—its yoke was fastened to the cart with thongs of leather in a complex series of multiple knots sailors called a Turk's head.

An ancient oracle predicted that whoever could loosen the knot would become lord of all Asia. They could hear Alexander going *schwing* all the way back in Athens. That no one in history had been able to accomplish the feat made the challenge irresistible to Alexander. More importantly, he needed another ego boost. Although he was flush with victory after his first battle with the Persians, Alexander knew that the Persian king, Darius, was gathering forces from every corner of his vast empire to go after Alexander in round two. Undoing the Gordian Knot to become lord of all Asia would be a huge psychological boost to Alexander and his army. He had to go for it.

When he and his peeps made their way to the wagon, a large crowd of rubberneckers gathered. The atmosphere was heavy with anticipation—in fact, Alexander's officers didn't want him to try. A Turk's head knot has no visible loose ends. How would he possibly undo it? He couldn't risk the humiliation of such a public failure.

Alexander tried for hours, but he couldn't untie the labyrinthine tangle. What happened next is any historian's guess. The only thing that's certain is that Alexander finally managed to untie the knot. Some people think he truly figured it out; others think he fudged just a bit, if you can call whacking the knot with his sword "fudging."

Now, cutting rather than untying the knot probably wasn't what the oracle had in mind when she prophesied the meaning of the deed, but Alexander never quibbled over semantics. A great cry rose from the crowd as Alexander stripped the leather from the wagon, took a bow, and danced the Macarena.

Thunder and lightning filled the skies that night, which Alexander and the seers believed was Zeus's way of signaling his approval of the king's actions and foretelling his great victory in Persia. The storm could just as easily have meant divine wrath— or that Zeus was clearing a little phlegm after a fatty meal. But no matter the meaning, Alexander had made up his mind: Persia would be his bitch.

Soon after Gordium's "vote of confidence," Alexander took over Egypt. There Alexander's already large ego ballooned into megalomania. The Egyptians, you see, made it official: They anointed him as a god. He was barely 25.

Amazingly, the Egyptians were grateful for Alexander's invasion. Why? Egypt had been occupied by Persia for 200 years. The

Egyptians hated the Persians, especially the Persian satrap (the ruling bureaucrat). He had drained Egypt's vast grain reserves and taxed the people to hell and back. Adding insult to injury, the Persians showed little respect for Egypt's ancient traditions. So when Alexander marched in as king by right of conquest, the people and ruling classes alike hailed him as a liberator and hero.

Alexander walked through the streets with his arms outstretched as he yelled, "Send me your tired, your poor, your adoring masses."

The conquering king hung out in the royal palaces in Memphis, where the priests warmly embraced him. (They had lost power under Persian control.) In Alexander they saw the possibility that their privileged place in Egyptian society might be restored, and they were right. They rewarded Alexander by naming him pharaoh (the Egyptian name for "Fairy") and giving him the double crown of Upper and Lower Egypt. And there she went, working the catwalk, wearing a gown and crown: Miss World Conqueror, 332 BCE.

Now why would the Egyptians so readily proclaim Alexander a Pharaoh but diss King Darius, the Persian leader who had ruled over them? Were they not both foreigners? Did they not both enter Egypt as conquerors? The key difference was that Alexander was smart enough to remember Plato's words: "In Egypt it is not possible for a king to rule without the priests' support." So he upheld all the traditional practices. He dressed in Egyptian clothing and restored Egypt's religious centers, including the temples at Karnak and Luxor. The payoff? In hieroglyphics, next to his portrait, Alexander was described as "Horus, strong ruler, he who seizes the lands of the foreigners, beloved of Amun and chosen one of Ra."

When someone asks you if you're a god, you say yes!

After Egypt, Alexander's vanity and ego were insufferable. It's not hard to see why. At an age when most of us are trying figure out what we want to be when we grow up, Alexander was already king of Greece, Egypt, and Persia. His success came with a price, though. Plots to kill the conquering king began to hatch left and right.

One plot involved a teenager—one Alexander had slept with, no less. Talk about killer sex. The would-be assassin was a page who was enraged when he was replaced by another sweet young thing in Alexander's bed. The page got others to join the plot. On the night the assassins were to strike, a Syrian seer warned Alexander not to go back to his bed, where the deed was supposed to take place. So he didn't. Instead he stayed up drinking with friends till dawn.

Pages being pages, one of them couldn't keep his mouth shut and gossiped about the plan. Alexander found out and did what any compassionate conservative might do: He had the key conspirator stoned to death in the public square.

The most dramatic example of Alexander's outlandish vanity came when he murdered Black Cleitus, one of his most accomplished soldiers. When Alexander was 28 years old, he hosted a party to celebrate ongoing victories, and Cleitus was way in his cups.

Cleitus was a mean, loud drunk. And he got particularly mean and loud on the subject of Alexander's father, Philip. Alexander, Cleitus kept insisting, hadn't come close to achieving what his father had. Now remember, admiration was like oxygen to Alexander. If adulation weren't circulating in a room he'd begin to hyperventilate. Cleitus couldn't leave it alone, insulting Alexander at every turn (dude, Chihuahuas should never bark at Dobermans). Alexander, also drunk and insane with rage, picked up a spear and threw it into Cleitus' heart.

Silence befell the palace. Alexander could not believe what he had done. Greek soldiers had the right to free speech, and Alexander had killed someone for simply speaking his mind. Worse, Black Cleitus had once saved Alexander's life in battle.

When Alexander realized what he had done, he took the spear out of Cleitus' body and tried to kill himself with it. Alexander lived his life according to the Homeric ideal, and in this ideal the only recourse for a hero who had shamed himself was suicide (think Ajax in the *Iliad*). Alexander's guards wrestled the spear out of his hands before he could do it. Alexander then flung himself into his tent, sobbed and wailed, refused to eat or drink, and didn't come out for three days. For pure theatricality, the man had no equal.

Alexander's generals were floored by his histrionics. They didn't think killing Cleitus was such a big deal—so what that the king had offed a loud-mouthed boor? They were Macedonians, for crying out loud! There were plenty more where that one came from.

Fearing for Alexander's sanity, the generals convened a posthumous tribunal and declared Cleitus guilty of treason. Now there was nothing to be ashamed of, they reasoned. Alexander had killed a traitor, not a soldier exercising his free speech. Unfortunately, their ploy didn't work.

Friends came and priests went, but no one could soothe Alexander. Finally, the words of a philosopher brought Alexander around. According to Plutarch, this is what the philosopher said: "Here is this Alexander whom the whole world now looks to for an example, and he is lying on the floor weeping like a slave, terrified of the law and of what men will say of him. And yet all the time it should be he who represents the law and sets up the criterion of justice. Why else did he conquer, unless it was to govern and command? It was certainly not to allow himself to submit like a slave to the foolish opinion of others. Do you not know that Zeus has Justice and Law seated by his side to prove that everything that is done by the rule of the world is lawful and just?"

The philosopher compared Alexander to Zeus and basically said, "Look, Zeus doesn't question himself about the rightness or wrongness of his actions. He doesn't care what others think. Why should you?" In other words, he who makes the law can't break the law—'cause you can just *change* the law! So quit yer bitchin' and move on.

This shocked Alexander out of his dramatic self-flagellation. What's fascinating is that nothing worked—not reason, not common sense, not the entreaties of his loyal followers—but an appeal to Alexander's vanity!

Alexander emerged from his tent ready to rumble. And rumble he did. He captured all of Afghanistan (which, by the way, no one has ever been able to do since—ask the Russians) and moved on to India. Why? Well, why not? He was a demigod—demigods could do whatever the hell they wanted.

At the ripe old age of 30, Alexander lay siege to the ancient Indian city of Bazira (in present-day Pakistan). The inhabitants escaped to the Rock of Aornus, also known as Rock of the Holy Man. This natural rock formation (henceforth known as the Rock) rose 8,000 feet above the Indus River. The inhabitants had water from a natural spring and arable land to grow food. Nobody had every stormed this huge outcropping; naturally, Alexander saw its supposed impregnability as a challenge. Plus, it was an important strategic outpost.

The Rock held a particularly strong appeal for Alexander because one of the legends of Heracles (we know him as Hercules because that's what the Romans called him) involved a similar challenge. Heracles, son of Zeus, had failed to take the Rock in a World Wrestling Federation championship match. So Alexander petitioned the WWF's governing body for a title-weight tag-team bout in which Hulk Hogan would take the fourth spot. Alexander received a polite rejection letter asking him to "call back in a couple thousand years."

Anyway, Heracles had also tried to gain control of the Rock (the fortification, not the wrestler) as he wandered the earth performing his 12 great labors. If Heracles failed, how could Alexander succeed? (*Curtains lift, spotlight shines, Alexander's ego enters, stage left.*)

From intelligence provided by Scotland Yard, Alexander learned that the only way to attack the Rock was to mount an attack from a nearby mountain. There was just one little problem: An 800-foot ravine separated the mountain and the Rock. Local guides showed Alexander that the only path from the mountain to the Rock was so narrow that troops would be forced to pass along it single file, making his soldiers sitting ducks for the enemy's arrows and boulders.

Alexander drew attention away from the ravine by having a battalion amass at the top of the nearby mountain while his engineers quickly built a bridge across the chasm. Working night and day his crews pushed mounds of earth into the ravine and slowly created a makeshift road using fir trees from the mountainside. Communicating with smoke signals, Alexander ordered the battalion to attack from every Greek's favorite position—the rear—while Alexander attacked from the front.

The Bazirian defenders showered the troops with arrows, spears, and rocks, but the Macedonians, with their awesome catapults and artillery, pushed their way forward and attacked in kind. Realizing they were dead meat, the Bazirians quickly changed their minds and begged for a truce.

As the truce talks commenced Alexander discovered they were just a delay tactic the Bazirians were using to plot their escape. So he rushed their position and slaughtered them where they stood. Many jumped to their deaths from the cliffs.

Alexander may have liked his precious bath oils and candlelit mirrors, but don't mess with him on the battlefield. That he was a son of a god could be disputed; that he was a son of a bitch could not.

At the end of the battle, a profound realization set in: Alexander had managed to do what Heracles, the son of Zeus, could not. If this wasn't further evidence of Alexander's divinity, what was? The fact that Alexander asked himself this question after every one of his accomplishments shows that his belief in being a demigod ran neck and neck with the worry that he was not.

Convincing his men that he was part god was one of the keys to Alexander's astounding successes. Alexander quickly followed up his capture of the Rock by releasing his international best seller, *The Seven Habits of Highly Effective People Who Think They're a God.*

In a world where gods were believed to take human form, Alexander became intoxicated with this exalted view of himself. This was especially true in bed. When his lovers yelled "Oh, God, I'm coming!" Alexander always replied, "I know, sweetheart, I know."

Chapter 3

The King and His Inner Drama Queen

There is no question that Alexander was at the top of the Most Wanted list at police headquarters, Drama Division. His gift for the overly dramatic gesture has never been equaled. Yet there was something unique about Alexander's histrionics—something that set him apart from all the divas that would come after him. Yes, he cried easily. Yes, he threatened suicide if he didn't get his way. Yes, he liked to punctuate every phrase he uttered with an exclamation mark. Yes, he loved to wear outrageous clothes. Yes, everything was an emergency.

But Alexander was a different kind of drama queen. Usually we think of them as the pumped, plucked, and pickled Boys in the Band. But as over-the-top as Alexander could be, he was no Liberace in fatigues. If you're thinking Paul Lynde leading 40,000 men across the desert, think again. If you're thinking Steven Cojocaru in hand-to-hand combat, you're deluded. If you're thinking Michael Musto slitting his enemy's throats with a nail file, stop thinking—please, you're giving us a headache.

Instead, think Patton taking bubble baths or MacArthur in moo-moos or Schwarzkopf with fag hags or Vin Diesel elbowing Aretha Franklin off the stage at a VH1 concert.

Perhaps the best place to begin exploring Alexander's penchant for the flamboyant is in an area toward which all temperamental divas gravitate: music. Alexander loved singing, dancing, and playing instruments. Many people heard him sing and play the lyre. As an adult, he was a great patron of musicians, though there are no historical accounts of his playing or singing once he grew up. The reason, some say, is because he had an effeminate voice. Others say it's because he couldn't throw a Vegas fan-kick and land on a cabaret chair without falling.

The Greek military historian Aelian said Alexander had a high-pitched singing voice. One day, as a boy, he was singing "You Light Up My Crack Pipe," Whitney Houston's cover of Debby Boone's hit, when his father happened by. Philip looked at Alexander like he'd just put Barbie's hair in a ponytail and couldn't decide which outfit she should wear. He immediately threatened the boy with an emergency nelly-ectomy. Alexander, shamed by the smear of effeminacy, never sang in public again. This is an important historical fact, for it points toward a central aspect of his character: Alexander was the manliest drama queen who ever lived.

To understand Alexander's sense of life as theater we must turn, once again, to Greek mythology. Remember, Homer's *Iliad* was treated the way fundamentalists treat the Bible today—as the literal word of God (or, in their case, the gods). Not only did the epic story teach men the importance of honor, valor, and courage, it also taught them the finer points of how to blow the smallest slight or provocation completely out of proportion.

In Greek mythology there are generally six classes of beings. In the first tier are gods (Zeus, Apollo, Dionysus), heroes (Achilles, Heracles, Ajax), and men (Philip, Antipater, Aristotle). In the second tier are men who think they're gods (Alexander, Russell Crowe) and men who think they're women (Dustin

Hoffman in *Tootsie,* Robin Williams in *Mrs. Doubtfire,* and Nathan Lane in *anything*).

Heroes distinguished themselves from ordinary men through supernatural feats, indicating that one of their parents was a god. Achilles and Heracles are perfect examples. As we learned in chapter one, Alexander's mother was said to have descended from Achilles' lineage. And it was Achilles, the star of the *Iliad,* that Alexander tried to emulate (he was even nicknamed "Achilles" by his tutors). To understand Alexander we must first understand Achilles, the mightiest of Greek warriors.

Achilles provided Alexander with examples of soaring deeds to emulate and hydrogen-powered catfights to surpass. Recall that Achilles got his power from being dipped in the River Styx, whose magical waters made him invincible. Legend has it that he grew up in the woods, eating the marrow of bears for courage and the sinew of deer for speed. At five he supposedly killed his first wild boor (a drunken disciple of Dionysus who tried to sell him insurance). Later, at six, he killed his first boar. He was said to have the ability to outrun wild deer at the hunts. Achilles grew up to be the bravest, handsomest, and swiftest of heroes. As a teen he commanded his city-state's navy, and he always fought on the front line in battle (often with his lover Patroklos at his side).

Sound familiar? It should. We just described Alexander's life. Alexander was obsessed with Achilles and made special pilgrimages to his tomb, where he left flowers, candles, and paper mache heart on which he'd painted the phrase 4-EVER. Alexander's boyfriend, Hephaestion, reportedly left a wreath on the tomb of Patroklos, Achilles' boyfriend. If they had all lived at the same time they'd have double-dated.

The parallels between Alexander and Achilles are inescapable: Both men were believed to be the product of unions between gods and humans, both had lifelong boyfriends who died before them, both led the Greeks against powerful enemies, both were considered the best fighters of their time, both were savage and savagely dramatic, and both died young (in fact, at around the same age: 32).

"Ever to be best and stand far above others," was one of Alexander's favorite lines in the *Iliad*. That explains a lot about his desire to play the role of world conqueror and his insistence on fresh-cut flowers in his dressing room.

Alexander was deeply obsessed with the *Iliad* and kept the book, along with a knife (required equipment for kings of Macedonia), under his pillow when he slept. During the day, he kept his personal copy of the *Iliad*, which was peppered with margin notes from Aristotle, in a jewel-covered gold box.

Not many people know this, but Achilles, the greatest of Greek warriors, pranced around like a girl and wore women's clothing. That's not a sentence the fact-checker didn't catch. Achilles used to sit in front of the mirror, brush his wig, and sing, "A little makeup, a little paint, will make a man what he ain't." Well, OK, *that* was an exaggeration, but the truth is that the he-man from Greece turned into a woman named Bernice. Here's how: Achilles' mother, being a goddess, knew that a great war was about to take place between the Greeks and the Trojans. It was prophesied that if her son fought against the Trojans, he would die. So she sent Achilles to the court of King Lycomedes, where Achilles was dressed as a girl and hidden among the king's daughters.

It was a good trick, but the Greek generals caught wind of his perfumed scent. The seer Calchas warned the generals they would never take Troy without the help of Achilles. As soon as Paris kidnapped Helen Reddy of Troy, the Greeks launched a war to get her back. Luckily, the generals caught Achilles at a karaoke bar in full drag singing, "I am strong / I am invincible / I am Woman."

Actually, here's how they caught him: Three of the generals, including Odysseus, took the red-eye to King Lycomedes' pad. There, Odysseus came up with a plan. He brought loads of gifts to the women's quarters and hid a shield and a spear in the pile. While the girls were picking through the bangles and bows, Odysseus had someone sound the war trumpet. Achilles, thinking the island was under attack, stripped off his women's clothes and picked up the weapons.

He was never any good at hiding his candy.

After pleading guilty to two counts of male fraud, Achilles was appointed general of the Greek fleet. He spent the next nine years sacking Troy's surrounding cities (the citadel itself was impenetrable).

When the city of Lyrnessus fell, its women, as custom dictated, were dished out to the Greek warriors like dessert ("Who wants pie?"). As commander-in-briefs, Achilles got the pick of the lot: Briseis, a royal princess. But Agamemnon, king of Mycenae, outranked Achilles. And since Agamemnon had to give up his own concubine to appease the gods (long story), he decided to pull rank and take Briseis from Achilles. You may as well have told Maria Callas the champagne and caviar ran out.

"Go ahead, Agamemnon, rob me of my rightful prize," Achilles reportedly shrieked, pulling on a smart cashmere sweater with a plunging neckline. "But know that the Greeks shall look for me in their hour of need and shall not find me!"

And so Liza with a *Z* flung herself into her tent and refused to come out, even as his fellow warriors perished under the attacks of Trojan general Hector and his troops. It was clear that without Achilles the Greeks were going to get stomped on like grapes at a Dionysian feast. But Achilles felt he had been dishonored. The code of Greek conquest dictated that to the victor go the spoils—not to the victor's boss.

With Achilles pouting in his tent, the war turned, and suddenly the Trojans had the upper hand. Achilles didn't care that his countrymen were dying all around him. He had a point to make and he made it with crossed arms and a tapping foot. Finally, Agamemnon relented and sent word to Achilles that Briseis would be his. Now would he please go out and smite some Trojans? In true diva style, Achilles said, "Kiss my ass." Agamemnon's men begged and pleaded to no avail. Achilles would have none of it. He wanted what he wanted when he wanted it. And "when" had already passed.

With the Trojans about to set fire to the Greek ships, Achilles' boyfriend, Patroklos, asked to borrow his armor. He figured the Trojans would mistake him for Achilles and head for the hills in terror. Achilles consented, but warned Patroklos to come back as soon as the Trojans fled.

Patroklos, wearing his boyfriend's favorite outfit, pushed the enemy to the very walls of Troy. The god Apollo, patron of the Trojans, stepped in and knocked back Patroklos. Then Hector, the Trojan Achilles, dealt the deathblow.

Achilles reacted to his boyfriend's death with a showstopping number that didn't leave a dry eye in the house. He cried, he wailed, he pounded the ground with his hands and feet. He grieved, he mourned, and he lamented. For Patroklos, one assumes, more than for the Prada he had borrowed and ruined.

When comrades brought Patroklos' body from the battle-field, Achilles would not let them bury it. He lay on top of it, held it in his arms, and sobbed helplessly. (This, by the way, was exactly how Alexander reacted when his lover Hephaestion died.)Nothing could soothe Achilles' grief. He purportedly said to Patroklos' body, "You had no consideration for my pure reverence of your thighs, ungrateful after all our frequent kisses."

Achilles finally plunged back into battle, routing the Trojans and slaying Hector, whose body he dragged behind his chariot.

Eventually, as prophesied, Achilles died—at the hands of Paris, Hector's brother. Paris of Troy pierced Achilles' heel with a poison-tipped arrow, which is ironic, really. When Achilles was wearing drag and hiding among the girls at the palace of

King Lycomedes, he reportedly said, "These heels will be the death of me."

Alexander inherited Achilles' gift for storm-the-ramparts fighting instincts and over-the-top drama. For example, he once grieved so hard for a pet he named a city in India after it. Admittedly, the pet was no ordinary animal. In fact, in his relationship with this animal—a horse—Alexander's theatricality first begins to bloom.

When he was a child, Alexander witnessed his father's men trying to tame a horse named Bucephalus. (After studying the second half of the horse's name, a team of Army linguists determined that Bucephalus is Greek for "hung like a horse." But the linguists were gay, so the Army fired them.) Nobody could subdue the horse or do anything with it. Disgusted, Philip ordered the horse taken away. Alexander told his father not to be a schmuck and waste such a powerful horse. According to Plutarch, something close to the following dialogue occurred between Alexander and Philip.

Alexander: "You're going to lose a horse that majestic just because you don't know how to handle him? Puhl-e-e-eze."

Philip: "Oh, and I suppose you, who's ridden, what, a couple of horses, can do what my men, who've ridden horses all their lives, cannot."

Alexander: "Well I could certainly manage this one better than they can."

Philip: "And if you cannot, what will be the consequence of your impertinence?"

Alexander: "I am *not* impotent. Ask Hephaestion. Gimme a minute with the horse. If I can't tame him, I'll let you have my entire *Powerpuff Girls* video collection."

Philip: "Don't make me laugh."

And he didn't; Alexander made him cry. Noticing the horse was spooked by his own shadow, Alexander took hold of the bridle, ran him toward the sun (thereby eliminating the shadow), threw aside his cloak, and vaulted onto the horse.

The group of men burst into loud applause. Philip apparently wept with joy and pride. When his son got off the horse, he kissed him and uttered the words that brought the audience to its feet and the music to a crescendo: "My boy, you must find a

kingdom big enough for your ambitions. Macedonia is just too small for you."

Is that foreshadowing or what?

Alexander's new horse's name was Bucephalus, which *really* means Oxhead, and rode him across Asia for the next 17 years. Bucephalus became a legend himself: His strength, speed, and courage saved Alexander's life numerous times. Bucephalus was once stolen while a groom was walking him through the woods. Alexander went nuts. At the time, the horse was 25 and would probably

be turned into a beast of burden. Alexander sent out heralds to announce he would burn nearby villages to the ground if his horse were not returned. He and his horse were quickly reunited. Alexander was so relieved he is reported to have paid the robbers for the return of his beloved companion.

Bucephalus never let anyone but Alexander ride him, which added to Alexander's mystique. He traveled the world with Bucephalus and rode him to great victories, including the famous battles at Granicus, Issus, Gaugamela, and Guacamole. Historians estimate the horse was 30 years old when it died, a remarkable fact given that not many men lived that long back then. Alexander buried Bucephalus with every honor and even named a city in India after him—Alexandria-Bucephala. Why the hyphenation? Why not just name the city Bucephalus? One word: D-I-V-A.

Every diva worth her wrath wants to be considered divine, and, as we've seen, Alexander was no exception. Early in his career as a conqueror, he requested divine honors from the League of Corinth. Basically, he wanted the elders to decree that he was descended from the gods.

Divine honors meant that the recipient had risen above the normal limitations of self-promotion to a point where the gods of public relations had to step in. To peddle propaganda as truth is no small feat (as any occupant of the White House will tell you). Charitable historians say Alexander wanted divine honors for political reasons. The tribute would give him more power, including the ability to bring back thousands of Greek exiles, reunite them with their families, and protect the Greek army from the use of disgruntled exiles as mercenaries in opposing armies. Less charitable historians say Alexander wanted divine honors because his ego grew so large he had to turn sideways to get through door to the horse stables.

Alexander loved the drama of victory—especially when the kings he conquered offered up something pretty. One Indian king handed Alexander his jewel-encrusted scepter as the Greek army approached, signaling his intention to give up. Alexander held the scepter aloft and launched into his victory speech: "I'd like to thank the Academy...." Like any good exhibitionist Alexander could find the dramatic center of any scene and play the hell out of it.

When conquered kings rolled over, played dead, and proffered something from Tiffany & Co., Alexander rewarded them immediately—usually by reinstating them as kings (as long as they pledged loyalties and royalties).

Alexander loved to hold court over the dinner table. According to Plutarch, "His custom was not to begin supper until late, as it was growing dark. He took it reclining on a couch, and he was wonderfully attentive and observant in ensuring that his table was well provided, his guests equally served, and none of them neglected. He sat long over his wine...because of his fondness for conversation.... As for delicacies, Alexander was so restrained in his appetite that often when the rarest fruits or fish were brought to him from the seacoast, he would distribute them so generously among his companies that there would be nothing left for himself. His evening meal, however, was always a magnificent affair, and as his successes multiplied, so did his expenditure on hospitality." Gay, gay, *gay*!

Of course, no one should mistake endurance for hospitality, and most historians don't. Alexander's "lingering" over wine was a polite way of saying that he was a total lush. More on this in chapter five: Married to the Vine.

Alexander's fixation with all things shiny and new rose to dizzying heights when he plundered Persia. Upon entering King Darius' tents, he was awed by the sumptuous amenities: gold and silver toilets, baths, and tables, ornate furniture, even a throne. He had never seen anything like it, even in his own palace. He is said to have uttered: "So *this* is what it's like to be king!"

They say drag happens when a man wears anything a lesbian won't. When Alexander took a look at Persian clothing, there wasn't a dyke within ten miles. As we've seen, Alexander loved drama, and you just can't have drama without a good costume. At first, he only wore the loud, colorful royal hats and robes at Persian events, but he couldn't get over how fabulous he looked in satin, so he started wearing his Persian threads to Greek events too. This pissed off his Macedonian men, who wished he'd have stuck with sensible cotton plaids.

They got even angrier when Alexander started dressing up like a woman. Yes, like his idol Achilles, Alexander the Great did drag. Some nights, according to the ancient writer Ephippus, he "would imitate Artemis, whose dress he often wore while driving in his chariot; having on also a Persian robe, but displaying above his shoulders the bow and javelin of the goddess."

To appease the butch tops in his posse, he'd sometimes slip into a lion's skin and carry a club like Heracles. Other times, he'd dress as Hermes—the messenger god famous for launching the first flower delivery franchise—and prance around in a kicky pair of winged sandals. This, according to Ephippus, he did only when he was "in private with friends," perhaps with a hit of Ecstasy and the stereo turned way up.

But if Alexander's men were appalled by the Bob Mackie knockoffs their leader took to wearing, they were in for an even ruder surprise. Alexander became quite taken with the Persian custom of *proskynesis,* in which subjects prostrated themselves before the king (or, at the very least, made a bow so low their heads touched the ground).

Many historians suggest that Alexander didn't dissuade the Persians from this kind of elaborate ass-kissing because he understood that allowing people to keep their traditions was the best way to keep the conquered conquered. And, hey, if the

Persians wanted to treat Alexander like a god—then let them.

Still, the Macedonians hated the practice of *proskynesis* and refused to bow down to their king. Greek kings always commanded respect, but they never demanded that you genuflect. This, in turn, perplexed the Persians. Alexander was clearly the king: Why were Macedonians not investing in knee pads?

The Macedonians criticized Alexander for "going" Persian. Were the Persians not the conquered people? You were supposed to plunder, pillage, and rape the people you conquered, not prance into their dressing rooms and see if they had anything in your size. Resentment simmered. Every time the Macedonians brought the subject up, Alexander put them off, saying, "I know we need to talk, but aren't these shoes just to die for?"

For putting on a show, Martha the Stewart had nothing on Alexander the Great. Consider his wedding to a Persian woman. It wasn't exactly an intimate affair; in fact, it became an occasion for a mass wedding. The feasting lasted five days. That's a lot of antacids—and, knowing the Greeks, several very necessary changes of the bed linens.

The marriage was a political deal to consolidate Alexander's power. And, of course, Alexander didn't throw a party—he threw an epoch. Alexander made 90 matches, and all the couples married the same day. He made sure his boyfriend Hephaestion married his new wife's sister. Why? Because he wanted their children to be related. Now that's love. A little twisted, but still, love.

Alexander started off the wedding by kissing his bride, then the other 89 couples kissed. Alexander was exceedingly generous, giving each couple a bed of silver. He reserved the gold one for himself. He wasn't *that* generous.

Alexander frequently played Cupid, firing off arrows like an Uzi. Eventually he legitimized—and paid for—the marriages of some 10,000 Greek men to Persian women. Most of the men already had Macedonian wives, but Alexander wanted children born of Persian women to be "official" Greek citizens. The marriage movement was also part of his grand plan to Hellenize the world—to mix Greek traditions and practices with those of the conquered cultures.

Another great example of Alexander's theatricality was the way he handled a near mutiny. Not only did he escape almost certain death, he did it with a step-shuffle-kick that ended up bringing him even closer to his men.

As the Persian conquest continued, Alexander knew he was working his army's last nerve. They were exhausted from all the fighting. They'd been killing after work and on weekends without overtime pay. So Alexander opened his vast store of loot and gave his soldiers bonuses even Enron execs would have envied. Plus, they were to be discharged and allowed to use their wealth however they saw fit.

The distribution of largesse backfired. Many of his men (some in their 70s) began grumbling that the discharge was just a ploy to enable Alexander to fill his ranks with the Persian barbarians they had just routed. At a parade, Alexander's voice was drowned out by furious shouts from his troops. It was the kind of tense situation that usually results either in the commander in chief finding his head on a pike or in the uprisers getting decimated in bloodbaths and floggings. Either way, it was usually bad news. Alexander would either die or have to struggle to keep his vast demoralized army, knowing they'd be ripe for future insurrections. But neither scenario came to pass. Alexander leapt from the dais into the restive crowd like Batman descending on Gotham. Hephaestion and the other generals followed him into the throng. Lesser mortals would have been mobbed and torn limb from limb. But not Alexander. Nobody touched him. He strode through the assembly and pointed out the ringleaders, who were led away, amazingly enough, without anyone coming to their aid.

Alexander then climbed back atop the dais and made the speech of his life. Many historians credit the barn-burning oratory as one of Alexander's greatest triumphs—right up there with the battle at Granicus and the time he wore a pink taffeta cape over striped gauchos without offending the gods.

Swayed by his confidence, his passion, and the curve of his newly waxed eyebrows, Alexander's men swore their allegiance once again. Renault describes the speech in her book *The Nature of Alexander*: "They could discharge themselves one and all; but let them first remember how Philip and Alexander had raised them from the poverty of mountain shepherds harassed by neighbor enemies ('of whom you were scared to death') to be masters of the world. It was a resounding roll of victories. He challenged them to name any wealth he had not shared with them, or hardships either. ('See here—let anyone who has wounds strip and show them, and I'll show you mine. I've no part of my body without them—at least, in front.') He reminded them that not a man had been killed in flight as long as he had led them. After a ringing peroration, he bade them go back and boast in Macedon of having abandoned him among the races they had conquered. 'You will be famous among men and a pleasure to the gods when you tell the story. Go!' He flung off the platform, rode back to the royal lodging, and slammed his door."

Drama? The man deserved a truckload of Tonys.

Alexander didn't come out of his tent for two days. The Macedonians hung around kicking cans, not knowing what to do with themselves. Then they saw Persian officials going in to speak with Alexander, and rumor had it he was replacing all of them with Persians. They imagined all their honored titles and roles usurped by the trained barbarians. The prospect drove them insane. A group of Alexander's men ran to the royal terrace, threw down their weapons and shields (the sign of surrender), and cried to be let in to talk to their king. Of course, Alexander wouldn't relent. He knew how to milk a scene. His men promised to condemn the mutinous bastards who started it all and pledged their undying devotion. They vowed they would camp out in front of his tent day and night until Alexander realized their sincerity and their hope for reconciliation. They swore that no man could lead them as well as he had. In fact, they had come to the realization that they were not led by a man at all, but by a demigod.

Demigod? Did someone say demigod? That brought Alexander out of his tent so fast the men felt a breeze. He came out weeping and struggling for words too—the drama queen. It was all very emotional. A cavalry officer named Callines spoke up. He expressed everyone's thoughts: By allowing Persians to kiss him on the lips—a sign of equality—Alexander seemed to prefer the conquered to those who helped him conquer. Callines was referring to Persian kissing customs. If men were equals, they kissed on the lips. If one was more powerful than the other, the more powerful got kissed on one cheek. If one was a lot more powerful, he got kissed on both cheeks. If he was even more powerful, he got a tongue between his other cheeks. Wait, wrong video. If one man was way more powerful, the others prostrated themselves before him. Although that's in that other video too.

Alexander had miscalculated. He wanted to honor Persian customs without subjecting Macedonians to them, so he had allowed the Persians to kiss him without requiring the Macedonians to do it. There was no Macedonian tradition of brown-nosing on the scale of Persian custom. But in "protecting" the Macedonians from this particular foreign tradition, Alexander had hurt them deeply. According to Renault, Alexander said, "But I make you all my kinsmen, I call you that from now on." This was his way of saying they were all his band of brothers. Callines came up and kissed him (on the lips, of course), and soon the line was out the door.

Alexander wanted a bigger gesture than kisses, so he called for a party with the usual mixture of melodrama and grandeur. Greek seers and Persian magi came to bless everything. With great pomp and circumstance Alexander assembled all the Persian and Macedonian officers and had them drink from the same cup. Thus, they kicked off an intimate cocktail party for 9,000 of Alexander's closest friends.

After subduing the Persians, Alexander's men figured it was time to pack it in. They came, they saw, they conquered. Now it was time to do a little shopping—at home. Alexander had different ideas. He was driven by "pothos," a "violent longing" or desire to continue expanding his kingdom. And he wouldn't take no for an answer. So he dragged his men into ancient India (today's Pakistan) for more intense, bloody fighting.

After a gruesome battle with a powerful Indian king, Alexander wanted to press on to what Aristotle called "the endless ocean" (the Greeks believed that the world ended at India's western frontier). The rubies, elephants, wild animal skins, and wealth tantalized Alexander. He looked forward to the campaign the way RuPaul looks forward to Dame Edna's garage sales. His men, however, had a different desire. They wanted to go home.

Alexander pressed through ancient India clobbering countless tribesmen along the way. Though his troops were disciplined, Alexander had failed to see how deeply their morale had sunk. The men suffered miserably under the endless monsoon rains. Fungus was literally creeping up their feet, their food was turning moldy, and everything metal was rusting. Hadn't they done enough? Hadn't they conquered the world? When was "enough" enough?

Alexander finally noticed their unhappiness and quickly mobilized to inspire them. It was here that Alexander won the nomination for his tenth Academy Award for Best Supporting Drama Queen. He called all his officers together and, with a great sweep of his arms, commenced the speech of his life. He had always been able to lift their spirits by recalling past exploits, plying them with liquor, recollecting victories, plying them with liquor, reminding them of riches won, and plying them with liquor. But this time it didn't take.

Respectfully, one of Alexander's oldest commanders reminded him it had been eight years since they set out with him. They were plumb worn out from all the plundering. They were homesick and tired of getting sick and dying. Tainted water and disease had killed more of Alexander's men than all the armies they had faced.

The commander gave a stirring "Let your people go" speech to try to appeal to Alexander's compassion. "Let our mothers take one last look at us, let us set roots with the loot and raise the next generation of warriors."

When the commander ended, Alexander's officers did not cheer; they wept.

That's the problem with understudies, Alexander thought. *You give them a little stage time and they think they're the main event.* So Alexander swung into full bitch, I'm-the-Star-in-this-movie mode and waved the lot away. He told them they could leave, and that he'd go forward without them. Then squeezing the dramatic tension to maximum effect, he flung himself into his tent with a great and mighty sob.

He kept up his pout for two days. Only this time nobody

bothered to check on him. As one historian said, Alexander's officers "answered sulk with sulk."

On the third day, Alexander meekly asked his seers to make sacrifices and read the omens. They basically said, "Dude, you'll have better luck making a successful movie with Kevin Costner."

For the first time in his life, Alexander drank from the bitter cup of defeat. No way could he take the campaign forward when the omens were as appalling as the weather conditions. Alexander relented and made plans to turn back. Suddenly he had his army with his again. Their anger vanished. They shouted and cried with joy. Sensing they needed to head off buyer's remorse, the officers described Alexander's decision to turn back not as a defeat of will but a victory of kindness.

Alexander could not have been happy. But he wasn't one to let it rain on his parade. If he was not going to get his way, then at least he'd not get his way in fabulous style. So he threw a huge party, staged games and horse races, and dedicated the army to the 12 Olympian gods. He had his engineers and architects build altars and towers to mark the end of their journey.

But like any good diva, Alexander got the last word. To punish his men for wussing out on him, he took them "the long way home"—a different route back to Persian headquarters before heading out for the Greek homeland. On the way, they fought vicious, brutal battles with angry Indian tribes. Alexander was almost killed when he took an arrow in the lung. Still, he probably thought the trauma was worth the drama. The guilt-inducing possibilities were endless—"See! If you hadn't made me turn around and go home, this *never* would've happened!"

In fact, he never let his men forget how they disappointed him. They were to be haunted by the tragic outcome of their bloodless rebellion against Alexander's ambition for the rest of their lives: Alexander—their wild, vain, beautiful, heroic, crazy king—died in Babylon while leading them back to Greece.

Some divas have their names put on plaques; some have their names put on buildings. Alexander put his name on cities. In fact, over the course of his conquests, he established 70 new cities, several of which he named after himself. The most famous, of course, was Egypt's Alexandria, which is still a vibrant, cosmopolitan city. During Alexander's time Alexandria was the greatest center of Hellenistic civilization and Jewish culture. Yes, Jewish. Alexandrian scholars produced the Septuagint, the first translation of the Hebrew Bible into Greek. It was through this translation that we came to know what "Alexander" means in Hebrew: "He who can kvetch better than his mother."

Chapter 4

Sex in the City-States

So was he gay? Depends on what you mean by "gay." If you mean was he sexually and romantically attracted to men, then he wasn't gay. He was gay on stilts. But if you ask whether he identified himself as "gay," then the answer is no. The concepts of heterosexuality and homosexuality didn't exist in ancient times. In that sense, asking if Alexander was gay is like asking whether he used cell phones or landlines. So, strictly speaking, Alexander was not gay. He simply had an unquenchable thirst for male flesh.

To fully understand the context of Alexander's love life, you have to understand how the ancient Greeks perceived the roles of men and women. Basically, women were baby factories. You either married them to carry on your lineage or you married them to acquire important things like territory, strategic alliances, and, in many cases, exceptional wardrobes. It's not that love didn't exist between men and women; it's that it wasn't necessary or even desirable in a marriage.

The biggest mistake people make about ancient Greek culture is to think they celebrated sex between men. They didn't. In fact, they frowned upon it. What they celebrated was something entirely different: sex between men and boys. *Paiderastia* was not pedophilia. Antiquity viewed sex with children with the same horror we view it now. It's just that their age of consent was lower than it is today. Back then it was around 13 or 14. Today, it's 18. Although at the Neverland Ranch, it's 12.

Paiderastia was a Greek philosophical concept that idealized same-sex desire. It was expected that older men would mentor younger men, teaching them how to hunt, fight, and take their places as noble citizens. And how to give a blow job that would make Zeus's eyes roll back in his head.

The modern mind automatically pictures "older men" as sick perverts in their 50s and 60s who hide in bushes and prey on boys. But the reality was that "older men" in ancient Greece referred to highly respected and accomplished citizens in their 20s and 30s. And they didn't prey on boys. In fact, they had to woo them. It was up to youths to pick their mentors, not the other way around.

The older man was called the *erastes*. In Athens the term meant "lover." In Sparta it meant "inspirer." In America it means jail time. The youth was called the *eromenos,* which meant "beloved" in Athens and "inspired" in Sparta. The partners' roles, like their poles, were rigid. The elder erastes (lover, pursuer, and active participant) and younger eromenos (beloved, pursued, and passive participant) could not switch-hit in bed. There was only one raging top and one insatiable bottom. However, the younger partners in the relationship knew how to work it. Historians recently discovered a shard of ancient pottery with an inscription that reveals just how sexually cunning the younger eromenos could be: "Grasp your older boyfriend from behind," begins the text. "Then place your fist on his abdomen and squeeze firmly until he coughs up more cash."

Paiderastia was a cornerstone of Greek society. Men in their

20s and 30s were expected to be citizens of outstanding civic responsibility, skilled in warfare, dutiful to their parents, virtuous, brave, honorable, and devoted to truth. Younger men, aged 13 to 19, commonly described as men "whose beard had not begun to grow," were expected to be athletic, brave, and willing to learn what their lovers could teach about life and the passions.

Paiderastia had existed for centuries before Alexander came along. Hundreds of ancient images depicting older men doing the hokeypokey with boys still exist to this day, as do literary references to the practice. Poems in book 12 of the *Greek Anthology,* for example, are almost exclusively devoted to the love of adolescents. Today the book is called *Freshmen.*

There's plenty of evidence that the Greeks believed erotic love between males made them stronger in battle. The bravery of male couples—as personified by Achilles and Patroklos and Alexander and Hephaestion—was well-known throughout ancient Greece and was an important factor in war.

If this tradition of man-boy love isn't enough to give today's conservatives a stroke, there was also a cult of nudity in Greek life. Indeed, nudity was considered a sign of sophistication. Civilized societies were proud, not ashamed, of their bodies and they liked to display them every chance they got. For instance, men exercised nude in gymnasiums. Yes, they had gyms 2,500 years ago. In fact, the word *gymnasium* derives from *gymnos,* meaning "naked." Imagine working the bench press and asking for a spot from a naked man. Unsurprisingly, the gymnasiums hummed with erotic energy.

The male body was so revered that participants in all competitions, including the Olympics, performed in the nude. At religious ceremonies, public festivals, and private feasts, young cupbearers were usually naked. And the main event at most festivals was a male beauty pageant, where men were judged for their

"manliness." We're assuming there were no evening gown competitions.

Admiring the male
body was so popular
that Greek officials
sometimes designated
homoerotic indul-
gences as a reward for
family men. The annu-
al Gymnopaidiai, an
important festival in
Sparta, was celebrated
with dances and per-
formances by naked
boys. When their pop-
ulation got dangerous-
ly low, Spartan officials
guarded the gates of the dick-dangling bashes with a strict
entrance policy: Only married men were allowed in.

Male love was so ingrained in the culture that many debates
centered on whether loving a boy was superior to loving a
woman. Boy love often won out. Phaedrus, a character in Plato's
Symposium, declares: "There can be no greater benefit for a boy
than to have a worthy lover...nor for a lover than to have a worthy object of his affection." The Greek ideal of beauty was not a
woman; it was a man. There was hardly a book, a painting, a
sculpture, a speech, a tapestry, or a piece of pottery that didn't
praise young male beauty. The word *kalos,* the masculine form of
"beautiful," was often carved into pottery that illustrated boys;
depictions of girls and the feminine *kale* were rare.

While *paiderastia* was a basic building block of society, it was
not without rules. Greek society passed harsh judgment if you

defied accepted norms of behavior. There were homo dos and homo don'ts: Don't shtup the underage, don't rape, don't prostitute yourself, and don't engage in sexual congress with slaves. A little senate, maybe, but no congress.

It's not that Greek males weren't expected to marry and raise children. They were. But they were expected to do something they considered grander—to achieve arête—and that required mentoring young boys. (We'd say "rearing," but that sounds dirty.) So the Greek male life had a definite trajectory: In adolescence, a young man was courted by older men and would choose one to be his lover. He was to reverse roles in early adulthood, courting and winning the love of a deserving young buck. Then he would expand his repertoire, along with his wardrobe, by taking a wife and having children.

Greeks encouraged man-boy love but discouraged man-man love. Why? Because they were obsessed with perpetuating the superior status of the adult male. That meant that the object of a man's penetration had to be his social and sexual inferior: women or boys. Furthermore, only women were supposed to receive pleasure from being penetrated. For young men, it was considered an indignity to be endured until they reached true manhood.

Adult males were expected to take the active, penetrative role in sex because their superior status demanded it. Sex was not a mutual thing. For the most part, you did not have sex with your social or sexual equals. It was all about the alpha male's power and domination. The shadowy side of this tradition was that misogyny ran deep. Greek society didn't approve of two grown men in love because sexual mores demanded that one of them take a submissive role in bed. And to be submissive was to act like a girl, to take on the characteristics of someone who had no rights, who was not educated, who could not hunt, who could not defend against an enemy, and who could not excel in athletics. A man acting like a woman was like a diamond pretending to be rhinestone. Why would you lower your market value?

The later Romans, taking a page from the Greeks (and there were plenty of pages who wanted to be taken), had an exalted term for men who properly engaged in homosexual acts: *Vir*. It symbolized the ideal man: he who penetrates other men but is himself not penetrated.

Any Greek man who wanted to be penetrated was unnaturally subordinating himself to other men. No "real" man could enjoy that, and if he did, he was constitutionally different and therefore unworthy of the status bestowed upon the noble male citizen. A man did not betray sexual and social expectations without being punished for it. To this day, thousands of years later, "gay identified" men ridicule passive sexual partners and revere active ones. That's why you'll never hear anyone complain, "There's nothing but tops in this town," or dismiss someone by saying, "Oh, he's just a big top."

So where did *paiderastia* come from? Where everything else in Greek life came from: the gods. Yes, even Zeus liked a little dick on the side.

Apparently, Zeus was looking for an intern on Mt. Olympus when he spotted the most beautiful boy in the world. "What's his name?" he asked of a mortal. "Ganymede," the mortal replied. "Ganymede Lewinsky." One day, looking down from his throne on Mt. Olympus, Zeus spied Ganymede chatting up some boys in a meadow. The king of heaven got so turned on he turned himself into a powerful, majestic eagle and swooped down to earth. Casting lightning every which way and turning day into night, he seized the boy in his talons. Up they rose, higher and higher, till they vanished into the blue. The sex between Zeus and the beautiful mortal boy was so hot, when they finished the onlooking gods had a cigarette.

Zeus was so charmed with the boy that he appointed Ganymede cupbearer at the divine feasts. Ganymede always kissed Zeus's cup before he filled it and placed it in his hand. The other gods completely approved of Zeus's decision. They rejoiced in having Ganymede among them, for his beauty was intoxicating.

There was just one little problem with the new Olympian intern: Zeus's wife, Hera Rodham Clinton. To make room for Ganymede, Zeus chased away the former cupbearer, who happened to be Zeus and Hera's daughter. You could hear lamps crashing against walls as far away as Hades. Hera, insane with jealousy, vented her rage by destroying the Trojans. Zeus, insistent, kept Ganymede on Mt. Olympus and honored him with a place in the zodiac. On a clear night you can still see Ganymede today, pouring nectar, shielded by the wing of the Eagle, or Aquila, constellation. He is Aquarius, the Water Bearer.

Zeus wasn't the only god who knew the pleasures of male flesh. Apollo, one of the most important Olympian gods, also lost his head over a boy. Apollo is associated with prophecy and the higher developments of civilization: law, philosophy, the arts, and decaf cappuccinos. Apollo fell in love with Hyacinthus, the young son of the king of Sparta. They hunted together in the woods and practiced gymnastics, something the Spartans were renowned for. Once, on a hot summer afternoon, the lovers got naked (big surprise), slicked themselves with oil, and competed at the discus throw. Apollo threw it so hard he cut the clouds in two. Hyacinthus ran to get the discus, but it bounced off the ground and hit him on the head, mortally wounding him. Horrified, Apollo raced over and held Hyacinthus close to his chest as his lover died in his arms.

Apollo's tears mixed with the boy's blood as it flowed on the ground. As a testament to Apollo's grief a fragrant flower sprouted, today called hyacinth, and on its petals you can read the letters "Ay," signifying the sigh of pain rising from Apollo's heart.

Handed down from the gods, the tradition of male love was an indelible feature of Greek life. But, as we've seen, only intergenerational mentoring relationships were encouraged. There were exceptions, of course, like Alexander. His erastes was supposed to be an adult male, but he chose someone just a year older: Hephaestion. Alexander and Hephaestion met when Alexander was about 14. They were practically inseparable for the next 19 years, until Hephaestion's death.

Hephaestion is described as a bit taller than Alexander and—get this—*better looking.* Considering that Alexander was so beautiful that drooping flowers sprang to attention when he walked by, that's high praise indeed. Recall the Cynic philosopher who claimed, "Alexander was only defeated once, and that was by Hephaestion's thighs." Hephaestion was the love of Alexander's life. Both young men studied under Aristotle. From the moment they met they couldn't stop philosophizing, playing sports, sharing ideas, or playing hide the hot dog. Alexander loved Hephaestion so intensely that he only had one other boyfriend, a couple dozen flings, and three marriages throughout their relationship. Hey, in Greece that was considered the height of fidelity.

Still, Alexander was not highly sexed, according to some historians. Certainly, he didn't embrace father Philip's screw-anything-that-moves ethos. He almost always refused the gorgeous slave boys and women offered to him when he conquered new lands. An exception was made for one exceptionally pretty eunuch named Bagoas. Still, he seems to have been asexual even where you'd expect a whole lot of wiggling and waggling to go on, like among his "sacred band" of male friends: a league of lifelong friends and advisors who had pledged themselves to Alexander. The intensity of their friendship would have surely invited some hanky-panky, but not one member of the sacred band ever claimed to have bagged the king.

In some ways, Alexander conformed perfectly to the Greek expectation of male nobility: He took an older lover as a youth (though he and Hephaestion were practically the same age), married by the time he was 30, sired a child, and eventually became an erastes to someone much younger—Bagoas, the Persian eunuch. He completed the classic Greek circle, except that Hephaestion never stopped being the most romantically important person in his life.

Words were everything to the Greeks, and they chose them very carefully. Alexander never referred to Hephaestion as his erastes but rather as *Philalexandros* ("friend of Alexander"), for he felt the word *lover* did not do justice to the closeness of the relationship they had. He called Bagoas his eromenos.

Alexander's hero Heracles also had a thing for boys. He was

unquestionably the strongest of the heroes, having killed two great serpents with his bare hands as a baby. Later in this life, he was compelled to perform 12 great labors as punishment for creating a little family drama: murdering his children. Known for his strength, Heracles was also known for his sexual stamina. Once he was the guest of a king who wanted him to diddle his virgin daughters—all 50 of them. That night Heracles screwed 49 of them (the 50th, dressed in corduroys and a flannel shirt, said, "You know I've got sisters. I want to know if *you* have any."). Nine months later, all 49 daughters gave birth to sons. The 50th was changing the oil in her Subaru.

But as much as he loved women, Heracles loved boys too. Ancient historians report that counting the number of Heracles' boy lovers required an abacus. Apparently, Heracles plugged most of the Argonauts, including Jason. His favorite eromenos was Iolaos, who was 16 and, more to the point, his nephew. Iolaos (pronounced I-will-lay-us) served as a helper in many of Heracles' labors. Heracles once remarked that his labors were easier when Iolaos was watching him.

Back to Hephaestion. Remember how he responded to Olympias' attacks? "Stop quarreling with me: not that in any case I shall much care. You know Alexander means more to me than anyone."

Alexander was known to speak just as devotedly of Hephaestion. When the two men first entered the tent of the conquered Persian king's harem, they came upon the Persian queen mother, who immediately bowed to Hephaestion because he was taller and better looking. When the eunuchs in the tent nervously cleared their throats and let her know she was bowing to the wrong guy, the queen, in great distress, quickly bowed to Alexander. According to Renault, Alexander said to her, "Never mind, Mother—you made no mistake. He too is Alexander."

Alexander's comment has multiple meanings. First, it tells us how much he cherished Hephaestion. Second, it confirms that Alexander thought older women were fa-a-a-bulous and believed in preserving their dignity, which he did on that and many other occasions. He struck up a terrific friendship with the old Persian battle-ax, as he did with many older women, a very uncommon practice. Perhaps it was the queen mother's name that made Alexander relate to her so well: Sisygambis.

When he began his conquest of the world, Alexander made Hephaestion one of his top generals, along with Craterus (whose name suggests he had a wicked case of acne). Craterus was apparently one of Alexander's favorite men—loyal, aggressive in battle, courageous in spirit. Unfortunately, Craterus did not like Hephaestion, perhaps because of Hephaestion's unblemished face. In any case, the men put aside their differences for the sake of the king.

Renault tells us: "Alexander showed more affection for Hephaestion but more respect for Craterus. He often said that while Hephaestion was a friend of Alexander's, Craterus was a friend of the king's." This was so not only because Hephaestion gave category-five blow jobs but because Craterus was more valuable to Alexander as a military strategist. Basically, Hephaestion was not so good at leading or orchestrating combat. He excelled in logistics and diplomacy, which were important but not as highly esteemed by the macho ancients as combat skills.

Alexander had three wives—Roxane, Stateira, and Parysatis. So that makes Alexander bisexual, no? Again, it depends. He clearly had sex with Roxane, since she bore him a child. Yet she wasn't a central part of his life. Not much is written about her. Alexander loved to shave, but this was one beard he didn't mind keeping. Alexander's marriages to his other two wives were strictly means to strengthen his cultural links with Persia. Stateira was the daughter of the former Persian king, and Parysatis was a scion of a powerful Persian clan.

Alexander met the other great love of his life at the end of his campaign against the Persians. Once King Darius fell, his generals offered many riches to Alexander as a sign of fealty. Among the invaluable gifts was a hubba-hubba, hunka-hunka, slap-yo-mama gorgeous boy named Bagoas. Alexander had been offered beautiful slave boys before but had always turned them down (something about Hephaestion hissing like a cat). But this time the boy was graced with incandescent beauty, and Alexander was smitten. Bagoas went from being the lover of a Persian king to being the lover of a Greek one.

A couple of years after Alexander conquered Persia, Bagoas won a dance contest. When he took his place at Alexander's side after the contest, Plutarch claims that "the Macedonian troops shouted out, telling Alexander to kiss him, till finally the king took him in his arms and kissed him warmly."

Bagoas had been an actor and a singer in Darius' court. He'd been turned into a eunuch to preserve his beauty and singing voice. Not much else is written about him. Apparently, some Greek historians conveniently deleted references to the Persian boy to protect what they saw as the superiority of the Greeks. They didn't care that Alexander was diddling a boy, but they cared a lot that the boy was Persian. Few of Alexander's countrymen shared his belief that the people they conquered deserved their respect. They were even more upset by Alexander's marriages to the Persian princesses. It drove them nuts that a Greek heir's blood would be spoiled by these barbarian sluts.

One story reveals a little about Bagoas' personality. Alexander had traveled to the Persian city of Persepolis to deal with a satrap who was on trial for looting the grave of Cyrus, a brilliant Persian warrior king whom Alexander admired. When Alexander first conquered Persia, this satrap, Orxines, had visited and sent fabulous gifts to Alexander and his court but pointedly overlooked Bagoas. His explanation? "I do not honor *catamites* (boy prostitutes)." After sending all the riches, Orxines awaited some kind of reward or gesture of gratitude from Alexander. But before that happened, Cyrus' tomb was opened and Alexander learned that it had been robbed.

Bagoas took Alexander aside and told him that the tomb had once been full of gold. Alexander often relied on Bagoas to tell him where Persians hid their gold since he had been part of King Darius' court. Bagoas lied like a dentist ("This won't hurt a bit") and blamed Orxines for looting the gold-filled tomb. On this "evidence" alone, Alexander condemned Orxines. As Orxines was led away, he looked at the lying, vengeful Bagoas and said, "It is a new thing in Persia for a eunuch to rule."

Meeeow!

To keep the political situation stable in his sprawling empire (and to avert a catfight between his main squeeze and his new boyfriend), Alexander dispatched Hephaestion on several diplomatic missions. His first assignment as a general was to find and appoint a new king in the recently conquered city-state of Sidon, formerly controlled by the hated Persians.

Although all sorts of ring kissers and ass kissers immediately surrounded him, Hephaestion took his time. He asked around to see if there were any survivors of the original royal line. He discovered that one descendant had survived, but he had been born to a peasant family and worked as a gardener. Still, Hephaestion checked around and found that he was a decent and honorable man. He sent word that he wanted to talk to the man about taking the throne and sent royal robes so that when he spoke with Hephaestion he would be dressed appropriately (Hephaestion didn't want to embarrass the man by drawing attention to his lowly position). When Hephaestion arrived, the man was not wearing the robes and was busy watering his garden. Hephaestion immediately proclaimed him king, shocking all the ass kissers. Why the choice? Hephaestion had found the one man in the kingdom who was immune to bribery.

Alexander survived a decade of war, mutinies, attempted assassinations, and battlefield wounds that would have killed lesser men. He survived extremes of weather and other hardships, fatigue and illness, and a 20,000-mile trek to conquer the known world. But nothing would compare to his grief over Hephaestion's death.

In Ecbatana, a beautiful summer retreat for Persian kings, Hephaestion caught a bad fever. After a week he appeared to recover. Alexander was presiding at an athletic competition when word reached him that Hephaestion had taken a turn for the worse. He left the packed stadium with no explanation. He hurried to Hephaestion's side, but he was too late. Hephaestion had died.

Depending on which historian you believe, he died of fever, alcoholism, or murder. Whatever the reason, Alexander's monumental grief resounded from one end of the world to the other. Writes Renault: "For a day and a night [Alexander] lay upon the body, till his friends dragged him off by force; for three days he could only lie weeping or mute, fasting and unapproachable...when he roused himself it was to wild extravagance of mourning. He sheared all his hair like Achilles had done for Patroklos (the usual tribute was a single lock, tied into a grave wreath). He had the manes and tails of all the horses clipped as well, and the ornaments removed from the city walls."

Alexander also had the doctor hanged. There was reasonable suspicion that the doctor had poisoned Hephaestion.

Alexander forbade all music across the land and he ordered mourning services in every city of his great empire. Teams of architects and sculptors were commanded to design memorial shrines and statues.

The only thing that comforted Alexander was the thought of dying and spending eternity with Hephaestion in the afterworld. But suddenly the fearless king was seized with fright. The fates had decreed that demigods could not share the company of mortals in the afterworld. In perhaps his most poignant effort to be reunited with the love of his life, Alexander sent desperate requests to the most powerful oracles and priests that Hephaestion be granted divine honors, which would ensure that they would not be separated in death. He sent a special envoy to the oracle at the oasis of Siwah in Egypt. The oracle, asked if Hephaestion was a god (back then people could become gods by achievement), replied, "No, but he was a hunk." Nevertheless, the oracle declared him a hero, a lesser type of god, and granted him divine honors. Alexander would spend eternity with his soul mate, though that reassurance did little to assuage his grief.

The body of Hephaestion was embalmed and carried to Babylon to be burned on a funeral pyre. Little did Alexander know that Babylon was to become his final stop as well.

Hephaestion's funeral is said to have been one of the most spectacular in recorded history, even surpassing that of Alexander, whose body was considered too sacred and too politically important to be destroyed. The funeral pyre alone cost something on the order of $100 million in today's currency. It was a 200-foot-tall ziggurat (a Persian pyramid) adorned with priceless Greek art. Ornate images of wreaths, eagles, torches, bulls, and lions were carved into the pyramid. Alexander even had beautiful sirens carved into the façade and placed singers behind them for the ceremony to create the illusion that otherworldly voices were emanating from the carvings. Parts of

the structure were covered in gold and others were painted with rare pigments. Alexander planned a monument that would have taken years to build. It never materialized, for Alexander died before construction could begin.

Clearly, the funeral was a consequence of Alexander's predilection toward the dramatic. But many historians feel that it also reflected a lingering fear that the gods would change their minds and separate the lovers in death. By creating a spectacle of mythical proportions, Alexander hoped to appease the gods and ensure Hephaestion's ascent into the blessed realm, where gods and heroes lived forever.

Alexander ordered that the sacred fires in the temples be put out during the burning of the enormous pyre. This was typically only done for the death of the high king. But recall what Alexander had told Sisygambis: "He too is Alexander."

Remember the gardener that Hephaestion named king of Sidon? This grateful king had a frieze created to commemorate Alexander's victory in Persia. The central figure of the piece is a handsome man on a horse vanquishing the enemy. It is generally accepted as the only surviving likeness of Hephaestion. Because Alexander died a mere eight months after Hephaestion, all the other projects that had been started in Hephaestion's honor were abandoned.

The only person who had been happy about Hephaestion's death was Roxane, who hated him intensely. Nevertheless, in his grief, Alexander turned to the diminutive and beautiful Roxane, known as "Little Star," who conceived Alexander's child during his period of mourning. As we'll see in chapter seven, Roxane eliminated Alexander's other wife soon after his death to thwart any challenge to her status as queen.

Alexander died not long after Hephaestion, just as Achilles' death followed soon after Patroklos' in the *Iliad*. So in both the scope of his heroic achievements and the depth of his romantic tragedy, Alexander succeeded in emulating the life of his idol. Importantly, any attempt to "het up" Alexander and Achilles inevitably overlooks the passions and motivations that made their heroism possible. If you try to straighten out these bent boys, you're getting the story wrong!

Chapter 5

Married to the Vine

Dorothy Parker once said she limited herself to three martinis because the first put her under a spell, the second put her under the table, and the third put her under the host.

Alexander would have drunk nine.

Alcohol wasn't just a party for Alexander; it was a career path. In fact, the consensus among historians is that drinking heavily contributed to his death. Alexander's drinking can only be understood in the context of Greek religion. In fact, as we've seen, nothing about the ancient Greeks can be understood without an appreciation for how deeply they believed in their gods. Every aspect of their lives was guided by these beliefs. And so it was with Alexander's drinking. Today we might excuse throwing down one too many by saying, "The devil made me do it." Back then they would have said, "The gods made me do it." A specific god, that is: the god of wine—Robert Mondavi. Or rather, Dionysus.

According to myth, Zeus rescued Dionysus from his dying mother (with whom, of course, Zeus had had a tryst) by plucking him from her womb and stitching him into his thigh until the baby was ready to be born.

Furious that he had diddled yet another bimbo, Zeus's wife, Hera Rodham Clinton, had the newborn Dionysus killed. A couple of Titan assassins tore him to bits and boiled the pieces of his body in a great cauldron. Luckily, Dionysus' half sister Athena resurrected him.

Eventually, Hera Rodham Clinton discovered Dionysus was still alive, and in a bimbo-fueled rage she decided to go after the brazen little brat herself. Zeus then commanded Hermes (the god, not the scarf) to change Dionysus into a baby goat and whisk him to the mountains for safekeeping. There, he was to be reared by mountain nymphs.

While he was living in the mountains with the nymphs, Dionysus took human form and developed the process of cultivating grapes to make wine. As he grew into his manhood (and as his manhood grew), Dionysus developed a large following of men and women who would venture into the mountains to worship him.

Known as "The Wanderer," Dionysus encouraged people to drink heavily and dance ecstatically. The word *orgy* comes from rites in which drinkers and dancers went into ecstasy and experienced a state of "oneness" with the Greek god. Dionysus was always accompanied by the Maenads—wild women, flush with wine, who draped themselves with fawn skins and beat drums in the woods. (Yes, the Maenads started the event that would eventually become the Michigan Womyn's Music Festival.)

When they danced, the Maenads often worked themselves into an ecstatic frenzy. They were capable of tearing wild animals to pieces with their bare hands and eating them raw. Dionysus' celebrations weren't always so violent, however; they also involved periods of deep meditation and extended contemplative silences. To skeptics this was known as "sleeping it off."

Unfortunately for Dionysus, Hera Rodham Clinton's spies

eventually spotted him. Afraid that the junior senator from Mt. Olympus would try to do him in again, he went on the run. Dionysus fled through Egypt, India, and the Napa Valley, starting cults wherever he went and teaching the locals to grow grapes and make wine.

Interestingly, Dionysus is the god who gave a certain king "the Midas touch." King Midas was walking in his garden when he saw an elderly satyr asleep in the flowers. Satyrs were closely associated with Dionysus. They had the face and torso of a man but a horse's tail and ears and a goat's horns and legs. And, most important, they had perpetually erect phalluses.

King Midas was kind and let the satyr sleep instead of punishing him, as other kings would have done. When Dionysus heard about this act of kindness he rewarded the king by granting him one wish.

"What'll it be?" asked Dionysus.

The king replied, "See this map? I want these countries to stop fighting with each other."

Dionysus grabbed the map and said, "The Greek city-states have been fighting Asia Minor for hundreds of years. I'm good, but not that good. Make another wish."

The king thought for a minute and said, "Well, then, I wish that Alexander the Great would stop drinking."

Dionysus let out a long sigh and said, "Shit. Let me see that map again."

OK, it didn't happen that way. Here's the real scoop: King Midas was greedy. He wanted everything he touched to turn into gold. So Dionysus did his best Barbara Eden imitation, crossed his arms, blinked dramatically, and—voilà—the king had the power to turn everything he touched to gold.

King Midas dreamt of being the richest man in the world. What he did not dream of was being the hungriest, thirstiest, loneliest man too, but that's exactly what happened. At first, the king loved his power. Useless objects became priceless assets at his mere touch. But *everything* he touched turned to gold: the food he tried to eat, the water he tried to drink, the daughter he tried to caress. In despair, he finally asked Dionysus to take back his golden touch. The god told King Midas he could wash away the golden touch in the river Pactolus. Even now the soil along the riverbank reportedly has a golden gleam.

After he managed to turn the whole world on to the virtues of wild drinking and even wilder sex, Dionysus' divinity could no longer be ignored. Zeus invited him home to take his rightful place among the other Greek gods. Hera complained bitterly, but she couldn't alter Zeus's decision.

Dionysus evolved into one of the most important gods in everyday life. He was associated with several key concepts. One was rebirth after death. This is symbolically echoed in the tending of vines, which must be pruned back and allowed to become dormant before they can bear fruit. The festival for Dionysus always occurred in the spring, when leaves reappeared on the vines. It became one of the most important events of the year. In fact, most of the great Greek plays were written to be performed at the feast of Dionysus.

Dionysus represented the double-edged sword of intense, ecstatic spiritual experiences achieved through mood-altering agents. On the one hand, debauchery was liberating and could lead to healing, communion with others, and closeness to the gods. But it could also lead to disaster when one succumbed to the insanity that often accompanies excessive drinking, dancing, and screwing anything with teeth.

So what does all this have to do with Alexander? Recall that his mother Olympias Dukakis was a fervent devotee of Dionysus. She met Alexander's father at a Dionysus festival (a glorious, blazing, barn-burning, furniture-breaking, rip-my-bodice, kiss-me-you-ebony-wench, grab-it-and-growl fuck-athon) and often led the Dionysian rites in Macedonia.

Alexander was faithful to Dionysus in every way and often made sacrifices to him—including his own liver. In his book *On the Death of Alexander and Hephaestion*, the ancient historian Ephippus described Macedonians as a people who "never understood how to drink in moderation." During official feasts that often determined important geopolitical events, the Macedonians were usually drunk by the time the first course was served. There's just no other way to put it—the Macedonians were a bunch of lushes. Whenever they passed AAers taking a smoke break outside of one of Hera's temples, they yelled "Quitters!"

It's not that the Macedonians couldn't hold their liquor; it's that they wouldn't let go. While most ancient Greeks diluted their wine with water, the Macedonians did not. Some historians think the Greeks did it to purify the water, others because it stretched the supply of wine, but most agree that the practice was meant to discourage excessive intake. The civilized Greeks, like the Athenians, believed in moderation, so they cut their wine with water. The boorish Greeks, like the Macedonians, believed in inebriation, so they cut their wine with more wine.

The archetypal Macedonian drinker happened to be none other than Alexander's father, Philip. Demosthenes, generally considered one of the greatest Greek orators, thought Philip was a "sponge" when it came to wine. Others of the age claim that Philip not only got drunk every day but that he often went to war half-cocked and fully cooked. Philip was famous for giving protracted drinking parties and winning drinking bets. He had a pattern: Kill men in the field and drink with them at the table. He was rumored to sleep with a gold drinking cup under his pillow so he could commence drinking as soon as he woke up.

Thankfully, Philip was generally considered to be a rather genial drunk, so his ability to drink like a fish was actually a political advantage. In warrior societies, where epic drinking was admired, Philip's alcoholic extravagance contributed to his personal mystique. The Greek historian Theopompus claimed that Philip used binge drinking as an instrument of diplomacy, winning over the pesky Thessalians "by parties rather than by presents."

Of course, his prodigious drinking did nothing to impress the Athenians, who sipped while he gulped and who longed for sleep when Philip would crack one open at the crack of dawn. Though Philip was impressed with Athens, he was not impressed with their prissy moderation. In the fifth century BCE, Plato outlined rules for correct drinking behavior, most of which still exist and are still flouted: no one under 18, only in moderation for those under 30, no limits for those over 40, and only water for soldiers when they go off to war. To say that this last piece of advice was seldom followed qualifies as a strong contender for Best Supporting Understatement of the Year. Almost all men-at-arms drank wine for courage. "There are no lack of examples," writes historian Jean-Charles Sournia, "where unforeseen defeats or victories can be attributed simply to drunkenness in the ranks."

Great. World history has been shaped through the exploits of generations of sword-swinging drunks.

Back to Philip: Friends and advisors who drank in moderation were often the targets of his infamous wit—like his general Antipater, who only tipped the goblet every now and then. Philip once said, "Now we must drink; for it is enough that Antipater is sober."

With Alexander, the grape did not fall far from the vine. As it had been with his father, soldiers admired Alexander's drinking almost as much as his heroics. Alexander followed his father into the bottle as well as into battle. Historians note, not without irony, that the son who tried desperately to distinguish himself from his father ended up just like him when it came to drinking.

There is some dispute among historians about the extent of Alexander's drinking, but there's no doubt that he had a problem. Plutarch claimed Alexander had a "warmth of temperament, which made him fond of drinking and also prone to outbursts of choleric rage." Plutarch here uses "warmth" not to mean "he was a friendly person" but to subtly point out that "he was a hothead who'd go cobra on your ass at the smallest provocation."

When relations grew increasingly difficult between Alexander and his fellow Macedonians while they were in Persia, drinking seemed the natural solution. It didn't help that, during this period, anybody who complained about Alexander was summarily executed for treason.

The Roman historian Curtis Rufus says that toward the end of his life Alexander "was spending his days as well as his nights on protracted banquets." But he wasn't drinking alone. He may have been a drunk, but he wasn't a drunken fool. He was making sure all of his officers were drinking along with him. Drunk commanders can't think straight enough to plan a mutiny. Still, Rufus says that Alexander's brilliant qualities were "marred by his inexcusable fondness for drink."

The ancients believed that wine didn't build character—it revealed it. One philosopher said, "Wine is the mirror of the mind." Callias of Athens wrote, "Wine is the test of character." If that's true, Alexander was one hell of a character. Between campaigns, Alexander held countless banquets and symposia. Usually the emphasis was on entertainment (poetry, dancing, food)—you know, the kind of sissy fare Athenians loved. But later on, Alexander's symposia became drink-a-thons that one historian described as "continuing until fatigue, boredom, drunkenness, and the violence of sleep intervened."

Whether the events were wine-drenched or not, Alexander insisted that his men recount their successful battles and campaigns. People could talk about the foibles and heroics of anybody at the party, but, when it came to Alexander, they emphasized only his heroics. If Alexander needed a separate chariot to carry his ego during battles, he needed a separate building to house it during parties.

Alexander's men bonded through this ritualistic drinking. If they didn't participate, their character or loyalty (not to mention their manliness) would be questioned. Alexander's vanity and insecurity ballooned during these drinking bouts. He constantly wheedled compliments out of his men.

Alexander also sponsored drinking contests at these symposia. The monetary incentives were so high that some men literally drank themselves to death. For some reason, Alexander didn't officially compete, even though he could drink the best of them under the table, and sometimes under the covers.

Alexander once held a drinking competition between the Greek city-states. In the final round, three contestants were to drink a bottle of wine in *one gulp*, walk into a cage, shake hands with a lion, then make love to a Persian woman who'd never taken a bath in her life. Naturally, a Macedonian won. The Athenian gulped the bottle of wine and dropped dead. The Spartan gulped the wine and walked into the cage, where the lion mauled him. The Macedonian gulped the wine and walked into the cage. Silence. Suddenly the crowd heard loud caterwauling. The Macedonian stumbled out of the cage, buttoning his pants. "Hey!" he growled. "Where's the woman I'm supposed to shake hands with?"

Kidding.

So just how bad was Alexander's drinking problem? He once attended a small drinking party hosted by his Thessalian friend Medius. Alexander drank a glass of wine to the health of each of the 20 guests then accepted the same number of toasts in return.

Is anybody else feeling a little wobbly, or is it just us?

Alexander is said to have wanted to drink like Proteas, a Macedonian folk hero who literally drank for a living. He drank such an astounding amount of alcohol people would pay to watch him do it.

This level of indulgence is all the more amazing when you consider what rotgut the ancient Greek wines were. They were thick, dark, and syrupy. When the grapes were harvested in the early fall the Greeks threw everything in the tubs—grapes, seeds, leaves, and stems (not to mention all the bugs that lived on the plants)—and stomped on the mess with bare feet. The unfiltered grape juice fermented in open vats, making spoilage a continual problem. That's why Greek wines had to be served *quickly*. But if the wine spoiled, no problem: They added herbs, honey, white barley, or grated goat cheese to hide the taste. *Yum!*

The Dionysian festival Alexander held about a year and a half before his death is the quintessential example of his excess. Imagine the scene: Alexander and his peeps reclined on a high platform slowly drawn along by eight horses. They drank and feasted continually, day and night. An untold number of wagons followed the royal table. Some of them were covered with embroidered canopies; others were shaded by twigs and branches that were constantly changed to keep them fresh and green. Alexander's officers rode on these wagons, and all of them wore tiaras of flowers and drank themselves stupid. Along the march soldiers dipped their cups, drinking horns, and goblets into huge casks and toasted one another. Many of them passed out on the roadside, oblivious to the pipes, flutes, harps, and singing. The cries of women in divine frenzies punctuated the revelry. It was like an ancient Mardi Gras, except nobody had to yell "Show us your tits!" There wasn't a blouse within miles.

There were plenty of ancient historians who disputed the stories of Alexander's drinking because they wanted to protect his reputation. Aristobulus, one of Alexander's top generals, claimed that the king stayed up all night drinking out of courtesy to his companions and allies. At one point, even Plutarch wrote that kind of revisionist piffle, but he recanted his soft-pedaling in a later work. The reality was that by the time Alexander was in his mid 20s, he was drinking like a sweaty buffalo and alcohol was transforming his personality from Dr. Jekyll to Mrs. Hyde.

Alexander became increasingly cruel to the inhabitants of the cities he conquered and even executed friends because of his growing paranoia. At one point he set fire to and gutted the Persian city of Persepolis. The conquering Macedonians were at a drunken celebration where Ptolemy's mistress supposedly said, "Hey, wouldn't it be a great idea to set fire to the palace and pay the Persians back for how mean they were to us in Athens years ago?" This, of course, made perfect sense at the time. Alexander was starting to believe that the problem with the world was that everyone else was a few drinks behind. So, in a moment of drunken psychosis, he agreed to the suggestion and destroyed everything. The city was viciously looted and burned to the ground. Alexander later regretted the devastation he had wrought, but, like many an unrepentent drunk, he blamed a woman (in this case, Ptolemy's mistress) for the mess he'd made.

As we saw in chapter three, one of the most dramatic examples of how the devil juice corrupted Alexander's wisdom and compassion was his killing of Black Cleitus. Though Alexander was bereft over this incident, the murder put an end to the liberty Alexander's men enjoyed in his company. This was a turning point in Alexander's style of command. Hatred and doubt began to simmer. Alexander was still genuinely loved, but his alcohol-fueled rage, paranoia, and insecurity began to alienate many of his men.

Eventually this alienation spawned talk of assassination. One plot against Alexander's life involved a group of pages, who were, as was typical of the time, only teenagers. According to Roman historian Arrian, the pages believed they were right to take Alexander out because his arrogance had gotten out of control. Alexander's murder of several key officers (including Black Cleitus), his demand that the Macedonians bow to him like the Persians, and his constant drinking were all sins that, the boys believed, warranted his murder.

When they were caught they received death sentences and were returned to their individual units to be tortured and killed. The commanders of each unit, knowing how paranoid Alexander had become, tried to outdo one another in their torture of the pages. In his last days, nothing said "I love you" to Alexander more than rending the flesh of the disloyal.

Alexander didn't just share his loins with Hephaestion—he also shared his bottles. Like Alexander, Hephaestion never got past the second rung on the 12-step ladder. Greek historian Diodorus tells us that Hephaestion drank like a desert marathon runner at mile marker 25. It was said that he once lost his corkscrew and had to live on food and water for five days.

When Hephaestion caught a high fever, Alexander, worried as hell, assigned the Greek physician Glaucus to monitor him, specifically instructing him to prevent Hephaestion from drinking. Nevertheless, on the seventh day of his illness, Hephaestion, like all good alcoholics, ignored the advice of his doctor (who may have gone to the theater) and washed down his roast chicken with a half gallon of chilled wine. *For breakfast.*

He relapsed and died. Alexander was crushed, and, like all alcoholics grieving the death of an alcoholic, he drank heavily to drown his sadness.

All speculations about the cause of Alexander's death point to his drinking as a major contributing factor. Ephippus tells us that at his last drinking party Alexander called for the Cup of Heracles, a six-quart tankard! After drinking every drop he saluted Proteas, the folk hero of drink. Alexander insisted on another go at the heroic cup. He began to drink and passed out, letting the cup drop from his hands.

Alexander's attendants put the king to bed and kept him under close observation. By all accounts he died in great pain, mostly due to symptoms of a disease like malaria, but his suffering was aggravated by his "overindulgence" in wine—if you can call taking less than an hour to drink almost 12 quarts of wine simple "overindulgence."

The man who conquered the world because he never took no for an answer couldn't say no to the one thing that conquered him: liquor. Thousands of years later, Winston Churchill uttered words that Alexander's ghost surely must have whispered in his ears: "Always remember that I have taken more out of alcohol than alcohol has taken out of me."

Chapter 6

From Ready-to-Wear to Ready-for-War

Sure, he had a great ass, but that's not why Alexander is called "the Great." He earned that title because he was a brilliant military strategist whose acts of heroism approached mythical proportions. In fact, it's said that hundreds of years after Alexander's death, Julius Caesar cried when he realized he could never equal Alexander's genius on the battlefield. Even today students in military schools study Alexander's techniques ("First you mount your men, then you mount the offensive"). Norman Schwarzkopf, the famed general who led the first Persian Gulf War in 1990, is reportedly an ardent fan of Alexander. Schwarzkopf isn't the only one. Most contemporary military leaders have studied Alexander's tactics.

Books about Alexander's military strategies abound. There's even a book on Alexander for business managers: *Alexander the Great's Art of Strategy: The Timeless Leadership Lessons of History's Greatest Empire Builder.* One of the chapters is titled "The Art of Deceptive Strategy." Turns out Alexander pretty much invented the classic military mind-fuck.

Describing Alexander as a brave warrior is an understatement. It's like saying Superman passed his vision test. This is a man who conquered the known world without losing a single battle, and he did it from the front of the line. That's right. Alexander didn't bark orders from a command center far removed from the battle. He didn't secure himself in heavily fortified headquarters, poring over reports and scanning radar screens. Even when his men were outnumbered two to one, he was on the front line alongside them. He was often the first person his enemies encountered and almost always the last.

In fact, Alexander was the last of the great military leaders to fight on the front lines. He suffered broken bones and terrible wounds and bore scars that testified to the fearlessness of his heroics. By contrast, the only thing today's generals suffer from is hemorrhoids.

That *any* man could be so courageous is astonishing. That such courage was embodied in a man who loved to share his bubble baths with his boyfriend is downright inspiring.

Alexander was an overachiever from the start. At seven, he entertained ambassadors from the king of Persia when Philip had a sudden attack of "war-itis"—something that flared up in him constantly—and abandoned his guests to go rout some enemies to the north. The guests were a little peeved: They had come to see the king, and who greeted them? A child!

The men chuckled indulgently, but Alexander was not a boy to be indulged. He got right to business.

"How big is your king's army?" he wanted to know.

"Don't you want to hear about the beautiful Hanging Gardens of Babylon?" the men asked.

"No, not really. How many mercenary fighters do you have?"

"Don't you want to know about the great king's children and their treasury of golden toys?"

"No. How long does it take to march into the city of Susa?"

"Don't you want to know about the exciting games our children play during festivals?"

"No, goddamn it! I'm trying to figure out how we're going to kick your ass all the way to the endless ocean!" Alexander cocked his head sideways, smiled, and waited for the answer.

Plutarch says the men were thoroughly charmed, much as you're charmed when you stare into the eyes of a cobra before it strikes.

The general consensus among historians is that Alexander was probably fighting beside his father by the time he was 14. Early on he showed the signs of a great sociopath: beauty, charisma, fearlessness, and an appetite for blood. As we learned in chapter one, Daddy Dearest was impressed enough with Alexander at 16 to name him regent of Macedon (acting king). While Philip was away, warmongering Thracians to the north of Macedon played right into Alexander's hands and attacked some of Macedon's more remote territories. Alexander could've waited for Philip to get back. He could've sent a small fighting force to subdue the troublemakers. But no. From early on, Alexander learned that anything worth doing was worth doing with great drama. So at 16 he donned his shining armor and commanded his father's army to follow him. You can imagine what the thousands of burly, grizzled, neo-Neanderthals in their 30s and 40s must have thought: "Great. Now we have to take orders from a teenage pretty boy. When's Philip due back, damn it?!"

But, despite their misgivings, they followed the young regent. Either Alexander had such a hot ass that people lined up behind him just for the view or he had an amazing talent to inspire his fellow men. We think it was his ass. Either way, he charged off to battle commanding men two and three times his age. He thrashed the Thracians. In fact, he so shamed them that they wouldn't show their faces again for years. How could they, really, having lost a war to a kid who turned their main fortification into a Macedonian military outpost. Alexander didn't just look like a Greek god; he acted like one too.

In fact, a recently discovered item from Alexandria's library of scrolls contains a parable addressing Alexander's youthful arrogance. Though there are differing translations, nobody disputes its essence, which goes something like this:

Achilles, Heracles, and Alexander died and went to Mt. Olympus, where Zeus sat on the great white throne.

Zeus addressed Achilles first: "Achilles, what do you believe?"

Achilles replied, "Well, I believe I was wrong to throw a fit, remove myself from battle, and let my fellow warriors die without me."

Zeus thought for a second and said, "I'm glad you're remorseful. Very good. Come and sit at my left."

Zeus then addressed Heracles: "Heracles, what do you believe?"

Heracles replied, "I believe in forgiveness. I know I killed my sons in a fit of rage, but I hope that the 12 labors I performed as punishment were enough to cleanse me."

Zeus thought for a second and said, "You are forgiven, my son. Come and sit at my right."

Zeus then addressed Alexander: "Alexander, what do you believe?"

Alexander said, "I believe you're in my chair."

Plutarch says Philip became "extravagantly fond of his son" after the Thracian victory and that he loved hearing the people talk of Alexander as their "king" and Philip as their "general." Father and son, as we've said before, got along best when they fought side-by-side—slicing off a head here, an arm there, and chopping the odd leg every now and again. The ancients had a saying about this: "The family that slays together stays together."

Philip wanted to invade Persia (he loved hummus), but he couldn't do it without a lot more soldiers, which he could acquire by unifying the Greek city-states and leading their armies to battle, and, of course, by making himself king of all Greeks.

Leaders of Athens, Sparta, and Thebes were not amused. They were damned if they were going to be led by a drunk redneck riding around with a confederate flag on the back of his pickup. It'd be like New York and Chicago being led into battle by Alabama.

Thebes mounted a full rebellion against Philip, who had made Alexander, at 18, a general of his army. King Philip and General Alexander marched together to attack the Thebes.

Thebes had a troop of elite fighters called the Sacred Band, which had never been defeated. But then, they had never fought Philip and Alexander. Father and son treated the Sacred Band as potential wine—a bunch of grapes needing the shit stomped out of them till they turned into something acceptable to serve with dinner.

Even as the city surrendered, the Sacred Band fought to the death. This impressed Alexander—though not enough to spare their lives, of course. But he admired their unbreakable spirit. He would later form a sacred band of his own with his closest friends, though a major label didn't sign them for years.

Humiliating Thebes worked. Athens, Sparta, and the rest of the city-states peed in their collective pants and swore allegiance to the he-man of the Hee-Haw herd.

Just as Philip got what he wanted—a unified Greece under his leadership—he was killed, some suspect by a conspiracy hatched by his wife. Many of the Greek city-states and barbarian tribes under Macedonian control rejoiced. The days of the barbarian tyrant were over! Munchkins poured into the streets singing, "Ding! Dong! The Witch is Dead!"

Philip's death created a power vacuum. Alexander rushed to fill it, with the blessing of his father's advisors. They counseled him to act carefully. The whole kingdom was threatening to blow up in his face. They advised him to use diplomacy before resorting to war against the other Greek city-states and the barbarian lands around Macedon. Alexander thought the situation through carefully and came up with a question that would guide almost all his future decisions: "Where's the drama in that?"

So Alexander attacked the other city-states with the ferocity of a Tina-tweaking circuit queen looking for one last bump. According to Plutarch, Alexander "was certain that if he were seen to yield even a fraction of his authority, all his enemies would attack him at once." He started with the rebellious tribes to the north. First stop on the Massacre Tour: Thessaly. It's here that we begin to see Alexander's amazing ability to anticipate enemy moves and change his strategies on the fly. This was more difficult without radios, planes, helicopters, or spy satellites to help him conduct reconnaissance missions. And there certainly weren't jeeps and tanks to transport men quickly; men, along with their horses, mules, and such, moved through terrain the old-fashioned way—on their feet.

The Thessalians quickly blocked the passage to their city—an impregnable mountain pass over a river gorge. They lay in wait for the snot-nosed 20-year-old general, knowing there was no way around them to their city. As Alexander approached with his army, the Thessalians commanded him to stop and informed him that they had not yet decided whether they would allow him to pass. Alexander agreed, as one historian put it, with "dangerous politeness," meaning that the spider agreed with the fly as a stalling tactic to get a better shot at it.

Secretly, Alexander sent his field engineers to cut steps up the side of one of the mountains (the side facing the ocean, which was completely obscured from view of the enemy). Without modern tools, his engineers and laborers were carving steps into the side of a mountain *by hand.*

Meanwhile, Alexander kept his advancing army facing the enemy as a decoy. Then, when the engineers had finished their work, he snuck a powerful contingent of fighters over the mountain. Before his opponents knew it, Alexander's army was at their rear. This was a position the Thessalian warriors warmly appreciated, of course, but they were stunned nonetheless. So stunned, in fact, that they surrendered without a fight.

Two months later—after securing allegiances from key city-states without bloodshed (they had heard of Alexander's savageness)—Alexander was leading his army through some Balkan mountain passes when those pesky Thracians decided they needed another thrashing. The Thracians had taken one of the summits overlooking a key passage. Lying in wait for Alexander's army, they lined up hundreds of big wagons and carts so they could push them down the hill and crush Alexander's men to death. This would only work, of course, with the element of surprise. But Alexander had sent spies and scouts, who reported the trap. He knew what was coming.

Alexander calmly commanded his infantry to open ranks to allow the carts to roll by them. Those who could not escape the rain of wood were to crouch down, link shields, and allow the carts to bounce off their makeshift shelter. The Romans would later be credited with coming up with this "tortoise" defense—think Russell Crowe and his comrades in *Gladiator*—but Alexander came up with the idea first. Needless to say, Alexander kicked ass and carried the pass.

As he moved on to secure his northern borders, it became clear that Alexander possessed a unique military gift: a penchant for brilliant psychological warfare. He loved to sneak up on and surprise his enemies, often flabbergasting them to the point of immediate surrender. Like the Road Runner, he would appear to be trapped, only to escape and prevail against his enemy in the most unlikely way.

In one march through a mountain pass, a band of Illyrian attackers managed to trap Alexander's men between a river and nearby hills. By any measure, Alexander should have been squeezed like a rotten apple: He was outgunned and outmanned. But Alexander believed in the thrill of victory, not the agony of defeat. He ordered his men into formation and performed aggressive military drills. In most cultures of the time, war was as organized as a high school cafeteria food fight. To see thousands of men marching with flawless precision—carrying 18-foot spear-tipped poles—was scarier than watching the Republican National Convention. The Illyrians had never seen anything like it before. Even though they were one in-law away from Neanderthals, they understood that their wooden weapons were no match for Alexander's swords, metal-tipped spears, and sarissas. They were so awed by the display of polished skill and murderous focus that they began to fall back. And just to be sure the resistors crapped in their furry skins as they hightailed it out of there, Alexander ordered his men to beat on their shields and yell loudly in a valley he knew would echo their noise, which made his army sound much larger than it actually was.

Meanwhile, Alexander kept marching north (into present-day Bulgaria) until he got to the Danube. While none of the tribes on the other side of the Danube had ever crossed the river to threaten Macedon, Alexander wanted to give them good reason to put any such thoughts out of their minds. The last thing he needed was neighbors with uppity ideas. He decided to cross a river nobody had crossed before just to scare the bejesus out of anyone who might consider it.

Easier said than done. The Danube was too small for war galleys but too big to wade or swim across. Besides, Alexander had a whole army to transport. In a fit of brilliance, he took all the leather army tents, lashed them together, stuffed them with hay, and transported 4,000 soldiers and 1,500 cavalrymen and their horses on makeshift rafts. For sheer ingenuity, the man was peerless. Imagine the production numbers Alexander could have staged on Broadway.

The tribes on the other side were so shocked and surprised to see his army coming at them at dawn that they immediately waved the white flag, or whatever the hell they did to signal surrender back then. All of the tribes up and down the river came to pay homage to Alexander and swear allegiance to him.

After securing his borders to the north, Alexander marched south to deal with the large and more powerful Greek city-states who were once again showing signs of revolt. Thebes in particular was a growing boil on Alexander's ass. Alexander didn't know it, but Thebes was in cahoots with Athens to overthrow the boy king.

He also didn't know that Athens was taking a "wait and see" approach with Thebes. As in, "Let's wait and see if Thebes survives a fight against Alexander before we throw our lot in with them."

They didn't have to wait very long or see very far. Fresh off his undefeated season (he was 11-0 heading to the play-offs), Alexander showed the rest of Greece how he dealt with traitors. He marched on Thebes and massacred everyone in sight, taking thousands of people as slaves before he burned the city to the ground. After he was done with Thebes, people talked about it in the past tense. It was now just a hole in the ground.

The other city-states promptly took notice. Now, instead of racing off to war they raced each other to the front of the line—the ass-kissing line. Mission accomplished. The city-states, unified under one king, contributed thousands of warriors to Alexander's command. Now he could invade Persia and get some decent take-out for a change. Why the obsession with Persia? Pride, prejudice, greed, and ego. The Persians had a history of putting on their wife-beater tank tops and slapping Greece around. Whether it was Greek outposts in modern-day Turkey or actual Persian invasions (they once sacked Athens and desecrated and destroyed sacred temples), there had always been antipathy between the ancient Crips and Bloods.

Alexander also exploited Greek hatred of the Persians for more personal reasons. Remember, he devoted his life to heroism and glory as defined in the *Iliad*. To achieve honor he had to do the following: outdo his father, bring glory to Greece, and distinguish himself in battle. What better way to do all of that than to conquer the hated Persians?

Alexander couldn't accomplish anything without a big, well-trained army. And you can't have that without a means to pay them. He saw the vast reserves of Persian gold twinkling over the horizon, and the die was cast.

Alexander convinced his countrymen that Persia was in need of "regime change." His greatest advisors—Powellus, Cheneymion, and Rumsfeldstratus—did a round of Sunday morning talk shows to convince everyone that Persia was amassing weapons of mass destruction. It worked. Alexander bypassed the United Nations and—with the help of powerhouses Honduras, Latvia, and the Dominican Republic—attacked the Persians.

In truth, the city-states were more than half hoping Alexander would get killed fighting on Persian soil. Then they could get back to the way things were before Philip burst on the scene. Hope springs eternal in the hearts of the naïve.

Alexander was 22 when he marched out of Greece into Persia. He would never see his homeland again. From the field of battle, he would establish his reputation as a military genius.

He first met the Persian army at the River Granicus, in northwestern Turkey. King Darius of Persia considered Alexander nothing more than a pesky inconvenience. Darius and his men sighed, rolled their eyes, and checked their fingernails when they contemplated doing battle with a guy whose voice had barely stopped cracking.

Fortunately for Alexander, there was no consensus among the Persians on how to fight him. This would be their undoing. You didn't fight antiquity's Superman without storing up some kryptonite.

Some accounts say Alexander's army outnumbered the Persian army. Others say that the Persians outnumbered the Greeks 20 to one. No one really knows. The only thing that's certain is that the Persians took the choicest spot: across the River Granicus at a point where the water was deepest and ran the fastest. Treacherous muddy banks doubly protected their position. The Persians placed archers and javelin throwers at the ready to pick off the Greeks as they crossed. The cavalry would mop up whatever they didn't pick off.

Alexander approached the Persians in full battle formation, ready to engage, even though it was late afternoon and his army had been marching all day. Alexander's officers were not happy. They paused as they hit the river and saw the Persians waiting for them on the other side. One look and they understood it for the deathtrap it was. Once they got in the water they would be completely vulnerable. General Parmenion, Philip's former right-hand man, advised Alexander to reconsider.

"Let's wait," Parmenion urged. "This water is too deep. We could find an easier place to cross or sneak up on them at night."

In a quintessentially Alexander response, he looked coolly at his general—almost three times his age—and retorted that he would be "ashamed if a little trickle of water like this" were to stop him.

According to Plutarch, "It seemed the act of a desperate madman rather than of a prudent commander to charge into a swiftly flowing river, which swept men off their feet and surged about them, and then to advance through a hail of missiles toward a steep bank which was strongly defended by infantry and cavalry."

Desperate maybe, but Alexander looked fetching in shiny armor and a helmet festooned with two bright white plumes. He couldn't possibly let an outfit like that go to waste. He took 13 squadrons of cavalry and plunged into the river to attack. Somehow they got across without losing too many men. Alexander and his cavalry had to engage in furious hand-to-hand battle as the infantry forces streamed behind him. The idea was to keep the Persians at bay while the rest of his forces crossed and regrouped into effective formations.

In these days of "heroic warfare," the leaders were the heart and soul of the men on the battlefield, which was why Alexander was so resplendently dressed. It was an inspiration to his men to see their gleaming, plumed, and plucked leader busily hacking away at limbs and assorted other body parts. But it also made him obvious to the enemy. Fortunately, the Persian commanders were dressed just as smartly, which made it easier for Alexander to go after them too.

Alexander moved his battle position to the right, making the Persians move men from the center to "cover" him (which was just what Alexander wanted). He faked left, faked right, and went up the middle with a long pass, charging the now weakened Persian center. The fighting was fierce and bloody. Alexander—on his trusty horse Bucephalus—plunged toward a key Persian general. The Persian hurled a javelin that stuck straight in Alexander's shield, nearly unseating him. Alexander calmly took the spear out, set spurs to ol' Bucephalus, and thundered toward the Persian commander. With a murderous yell he stabbed his opponent with such force his spear broke off in his hands when the tip lodged in the general's breastplate. According to historian Diodorus, "adjacent ranks in both armies cried out at the superlative display of prowess." It's the fantasy of every quarter-back: The opposing team calls a time-out to marvel at his pass completion in slow motion.

Stunned, but not out, the Persian general removed the spear and drew his sword for a face-to-face battle with the blond bombshell. But Alexander had no patience for that—he jabbed his broken spear into the general's face. So intent was he on killing the Persian general in command, he didn't notice the swarm of Persians coming at him. One Persian nobleman rode by on his horse and slammed Alexander on the head with his sword, splitting his helmet in two and cutting into his scalp. Dazed and bloody, Alexander was now vulnerable.

Another Persian came up to deliver the deathblow, but as he raised his scimitar, Black Cleitus (whom Alexander would murder six years later in a drunken rage) cut the man's arm off just in the nick of time.

Alexander fainted for a moment from the blood loss, then he managed to stagger to his horse and get on. Seeing their leader back on his horse gave the Greeks a huge surge of hope. They pressed forward as the Persians fell back. The Greek phalanx and cavalry hemmed in the enemy, and the battle turned from stalemate to slaughter. All of the Persian commanders were slain (including Darius' son-in-law), though many in the cavalry escaped, running for their lives. The boy king had won his first battle against Darius. Persia was well on its way to becoming his bitch.

After the battle, Alexander buried the fallen Greeks with full military honors. Then he visited with the injured for hours, speaking to each man and encouraging him to boast of his own bravery. The men loved the attention. Imagine Rocky Marciano complimenting you on your right hook. What would you say if he asked you to join him in more fights? That's exactly what Alexander did. He appealed to his men's vanity to make them want to wage more war. Alexander advanced rapidly through Persia after the battle at Granicus. There were hardly any military leaders left to organize a resistance.

King Darius was now paying attention. One year after the victory at Granicus, Darius had assembled a massive force to go after Alexander. Some historians say the force numbered 100,000; others, more than *half a million*. Either way, they vastly outnumbered Alexander, who had about 40,000 men.

Alexander expected Darius to come from Babylon and meet him head on. But Darius had other plans. He swung around and came up from *behind* Alexander, using the Greek king's sneakiness against him (imagine Wile E. Coyote tiptoeing behind the unsuspecting Road Runner).

Darius was also shockingly vicious as he trailed Alexander. Alexander had left his injured fighters in infirmaries at various outposts. As Darius advanced, he killed all the Greeks he came upon—in some instances chopping them to pieces as they lay in their beds.

Darius disrupted Alexander's famous logistic system and wreaked havoc with the Greeks' supply lines. By the time Alexander figured out what Darius was up to, it was too late. The Greeks were trapped like caged animals. It looked like it was curtains for the kid. His men had marched 70 miles in two days. They were wet, exhausted, far away from home, and vastly outnumbered.

All the Persians had to do was hold the line. A protracted battle would've decimated Alexander's men. But they underestimated Alexander's unequalled ability to whip his men into blood frenzy. Alexander rode his horse up and down the line, encouraging his men, recounting their personal victories, and calling each of his thousands of soldiers by name. (Roman historians in particular marveled at Alexander's gift of recall.)

After rallying their spirits, Alexander made sure all his men got a good hot meal and some rest, then he marched them to a commanding position overlooking Darius and his army. At dawn they descended toward the plain of Issus.

As at Granicus, the Persians took a defensive position across a river and lay in wait for the boy king. Alexander deployed a front three miles long. Darius—in his great ornamented chariot—was flanked by elite troops, who were in turn surrounded by infantry, archers, and cavalry. Alexander, on the right end of the line, figured that Darius would move his cavalry to "cover" Alexander. He guessed wrong. He saw that Darius was placing his cavalry to his left, where General Parmenion stationed his troops. He also began getting reports that some of the Persians had circled to the hills behind them. Alexander sent troops to deal with the ones behind them and, in a lightning-quick adjustment of strategy, changed formations to strengthen his left. But now his right was weakened. Hidden by the infantry at the front lines, he sent a con-

tingent of archers to strengthen his right wing. It was a game of military chess.

Alexander had hoped that the Persians would attack, but their defensive position was too good. They were forcing Alexander's hand. He would have to attack—once again, crossing water to get to them. His foot soldiers were going to be sitting ducks if they hit the water first, so the onus was on the cavalry, with Alexander leading the charge.

Once again, Alexander's fearlessness set the tone. Through the mud and spray, his advancing cavalry probably looked like crazed, foaming beasts from hell. Psychologically, the front lines of Darius' army were finished the minute they saw the wave of men on horses thundering their way. Darius may have had more men in the fight, but Alexander had more fight in his men. His cavalry demolished the Persian line in minutes.

Alexander thundered toward Darius. Killing him would not just end the battle but the entire war. But equally strong royal bodyguards blocked his surge. Alexander was cut badly in the thigh. (Worse, there was a run in his stocking.) Still, he pressed on. Darius' chariot horses began to rear and panic at the bloody melee around them. Darius took the reins and was trying to control them when another Persian came by with a lighter, smaller chariot. Terrified of being captured, King Darius jumped into it and fled.

Seeing Darius retreat enraged Alexander, who held cowardice beneath contempt. Better to die in battle than to live as a wimp. But just as he started to go after the Persian king, he got word that his phalanx badly needed him. Reluctantly, he turned and swung his entire right wing to support the center and left wings of his struggling troops.

The Persians, demoralized at seeing their leader run like there was a clearance sale at Nordstrom, lost their momentum. From that point on, it was a total rout. Once Alexander's phalanx was back in command of the situation, Alexander set off after Darius. But the great Persian wuss had a half mile head start, and the exit lanes were blocked by panicked Persian fighters trying to get the hell out of the way. Still, Alexander gave chase for 25 miles before letting Darius go. He went back to his men to celebrate their victory. From the first volley of Persian arrows to their triumph, the most decisive and influential battle of Alexander's career lasted less than *one hour.*

Alexander decided to let Darius stew in the shameful knowledge that he had run—*run!*—from battle. Any respect he had for

Darius was gone. In his eyes, this was the lowest of the low. No true warrior or hero would do such a thing. All of western Persia now belonged to Alexander.

It was after the battle at Issus that Alexander acquired his new boy toy: Darius' eunuch, Bagoas. He also held hostage the harem, which included the king's mother, wife, and children. Darius kept sending Alexander letters demanding his family back. Alexander would yawn and check his cuticles. At one point, Darius sent him a letter offering a ransom for his family and a treaty giving him a huge portion of Persia. Alexander's response? "Puhl-e-e-eze, you can't offer me what I've already taken."

According to classics scholar Peter Green, this is how he ended his response to Darius: "In the future, let any communication you wish to make with me be addressed to the king of all Asia. Do not write to me as an equal. Everything you possess is now mine; so if you should want anything, let me know in proper terms, or I shall take steps to deal with you as a criminal. If, on the other hand, you wish to dispute the throne, stand and fight for it and do not run away. Wherever you may hide yourself, be sure I shall seek you out."

Darius' cowardice just stuck in Alexander's craw. Still, the great wuss wouldn't let up. He offered Alexander an even larger amount of treasure, the hand of his daughter, and title to all of Persia west of the Euphrates. For 500 years Roman emperors would be content with that territory. Parmenion, Alexander's second in command, was so impressed he beseeched the king to accept Darius' offer.

As historian Robin Lane Fox relates it: "I would accept," said Parmenion, "if I were Alexander."

"So would I," replied Alexander, "if I were Parmenion."

But he wasn't, and he didn't. Alexander was not going to be bribed out of his glory.

Alexander would not meet Darius on the battlefield again for two years. He spent the interim getting crowned pharaoh in Egypt (pretty heady stuff for a 24-year-old) and subduing other pockets of resistance along the Mediterranean coast. One of these battles involved the siege of Tyre in modern Lebanon. And it was here that Alexander demonstrated his true military genius. He also demonstrated his characteristic stubbornness. It would take almost a year to conquer Tyre—an island city (with impregnable walls 150 feet high) that was a critical naval and commercial port between Persia and Egypt—and it would prove to be one of the most grueling military operations of Alexander's career.

When Alexander's army approached Tyre, the Tyrian king and his cohorts came out bearing gifts and speaking pretty words about their allegiance to Alexander. But they had their fingers crossed behind their backs, along with their swords. They had no intention of handing their city over to Alexander. When he asked to hold a religious ceremony inside the city gates, they showed their true colors and refused. Only a Tyrian king could do that, they replied. They might as well have lit a match near a gas leak.

Enraged but ever practical, Alexander huddled with his generals. Lacking naval support, he figured the only way they could take the city would be to storm it. So he decided to build a causeway; he put his engineers on the task. There was plenty of stone and timber available, and he used thousands of laborers from nearby villages to build a bridge over waters he would trouble.

The Tyrians harassed the workers with arrows and stones, but that didn't deter the Macedonians. As the causeway hit deep water, the trouble started. Persian naval forces arrived to pick off the workers and set fire to their efforts. It was touch and go for a while, until Greek naval support came on the scene. As

Alexander's men finished the causeway, the Tyrians fought with desperate courage. Alexander's army bombarded their city walls using boulders hurled from catapults, ships with battering rams, and siege towers with drawbridges.

The fighting went on for three months. The desperate Tyrians came up with a powerful and gruesome weapon. They cooked sand in giant cauldrons and poured the red-hot grains down on the attacking Macedonians as they tried to scale the city walls. The burning sand, which got trapped between skin and armor, was beyond torturous. Many men were lost as they hurled themselves into the sea to relieve the pain.

By the time Alexander broke through, his rage at the Tyrians had spiraled out of control. As happened often when Alexander lost his temper, blood was the only thing that would appease him. He destroyed the Tyrian army, butchered close to 6,000 of the city's inhabitants, tortured or killed 2,000 others on the mainland, and enslaved 30,000 Tyrian citizens. Talk about having a bad day at the office.

Alexander marched back into central Persia as pharaoh of Egypt and destroyer of the Persian navy. Meanwhile, Darius had used the two years since his disastrous loss at Issus to amass a large army and prepare for another face-off. Once again, Darius picked the location. And once again, he assembled an army that dwarfed the size of Alexander's. The Macedonians had close to 50,000 men. The ancient historian Arrian claims the Persians had as many as one million men. The two armies met at Gaugamela on a wide plain that gave Darius every home-field advantage. Like before, the Persians lay in wait for Alexander's advancing troops.

The Greeks were starting to fray around the edges. The siege at Tyre had worn them out badly. Yet, as always, Alexander managed to rouse their passions and focus their frustrations on the enemy (and, conveniently, away from him). As they crested the hill and saw the size of Darius' army, even Alexander was taken aback. As they set up camp, Alexander paced, trying to come up with a plan to deal with the outrageous way in which they were outnumbered. The old general Parmenion suggested a surprise night attack, but Alexander refused. Too risky.

Nevertheless the king of the royal mind-fuck carefully "leaked" plans that a night attack was imminent. So Darius and his men stood guard all night waiting for the signal that the "surprise" attack was coming. With adrenaline pumping and spears poised, Darius' men waited for the onslaught. And waited. And waited.

And waited and waited.

Meanwhile, knowing that Darius' men were on the watch all night for an attack that would never come, Alexander retired for the night and slept soundly. But not before composing his now famous blues line about psychological warfare: "If the attack ain't coming, it's me."

At dawn, Alexander marched down into the plain. Darius' men were pissed, grouchy, and sleep deprived. As he advanced, Alexander kept changing formation to confuse the tired Persians. Keeping his best general, Parmenion, on the left, he kept his line pulling to the right, where the horses and chariots could not run. Darius kept following, even as his satrap Bessus tried to encircle the Macedonians on the left wing. This left a weak spot in the Persian center (would Darius never learn?) and Alexander and his cavalry plunged in. They quickly fought their way to Darius. The satrap Bessus, seeing the Persian center begin to collapse, called for a retreat. As Alexander's cavalry closed in on Darius, the great weenie turned tail and ran. Again! Some men drink from the fountain of courage; Darius only gargled. It was a complete victory for Alexander.

Alexander's contempt for Darius was now beyond compare. He would later pursue the satrap Bessus, who overthrew and then killed the impotent Darius. But Bessus didn't make it easy on Alexander, who followed the satrap through the icy heights of the Hindu Kush. According to Renault: "Historians have agreed that as a feat of leadership and endurance, it far surpasses Hannibal's crossing of the Alps. Its hardships were to a great extent foreseeable; he must have felt an unshaken confidence in his men's devotion, which events confirmed. He may not have allowed enough for altitude. Provisions ran short, wheeled transport was impossible, and the ground grew only alpine herbs; dead mules were eaten raw for lack of cooking fuel; the glare caused snow blindness, and at 11,000-odd feet there must have been some mountain sickness. But Alexander was always to be seen as cold and hungry as anyone, stopping for a joke or to haul some numbed man out of a drift."

Bessus kept stripping the land as Alexander approached, but Alexander kept coming, leaner and meaner. He cast a spell on his enemies. Alexander's pursuit of Bessus, who dreamt of succeeding Darius, was relentless, and he was spooked. Finally, Bessus lost his nerve and retreated across the river Oxus, burning boats behind him.

The city of Oxus did not resist Alexander. There he rested and fed his men. Once strengthened he got ready to cross the desert, "exchanging a cold hell for a hot one," writes Renault.

His men suffered greatly while crossing the desert. Their water supplies were rapidly depleted. Some porters had found a water hole and filled a skin for their children. They passed Alexander, who was sweltering, and offered him a cup. Alexander refused, telling them he would not drink until there was enough for everyone. This was a typical example of his peerless leadership.

When they finally camped, Alexander refused to eat or rest until all the soldiers had done so. Is there any question why he inspired such loyalty among his men? The ordinary army soldier couldn't help but be impressed. Alexander slept in a tent like them. He knew their names, honored their accomplishments, fronted them in battles, and he would not eat or drink unless they had done so first.

Meanwhile, Bessus' support was waning. The people in most of the cities along the way preferred Alexander as their leader. Two of Bessus' chiefs decided to call it a day and sent word to Alexander to let him know where he could find Bessus.

Once captured, Bessus was stripped (a disgrace for Persians), his hands were tied behind him, and he was left on the side of the road. When Alexander's chariot reached him, Alexander asked why he had betrayed his king (who was also his brother). If Bessus had shown courage and dignity, Alexander might have shown mercy. After all, Alexander had pardoned and absorbed into his army a group of rebels he had seen courageously walking to their execution.

Bessus, however, whined that others were to blame for the murder of Darius. Disgusted, Alexander ordered Bessus flogged and sent to Persia in chains for a trial. At the trial Bessus' nose and ear tips were cut off—the Persian mark of a criminal. He was later executed by being impaled on a cross. (Mel Gibson has first options on the movie.) Bessus' body was then cut up and fed to wild beasts. All of this was supervised by a man who afterward pledged his loyalty to Alexander: Bessus' other brother.

Alexander spent the following months mopping up pockets of Persian resistance, sacking some cities, burning others to the ground, drinking until he was stupid, and, occasionally, murdering an old friend (sometimes all on the same night). But there was nothing like another battle to keep his men's minds off the fact that they hadn't been on Greek soil in eight years. And there were *always* other battles.

As Alexander marched into Afghanistan, the central northern border of the Persian empire, some of the local governors balked at their new king. One of these was a man called Oxyartes, who, along with his wife and daughters and 30,000 of his closest friends, took refuge on the Sogdian Rock, a supposedly impregnable fortress. While the storming of Sogdian Rock wasn't a key battle, it does illustrate an essential principle of Alexander's personal psychology: Never, ever tell him something is impossible. Alexander took one look at this towering outcropping of rock and demanded that Oxyartes and his defenders negotiate with him. They just laughed. "You're wasting your time," they scoffed down at him. "You can only get us with soldiers who have wings." Another note to clueless satraps: Never, ever laugh at Alexander.

Alexander called out to his men for expert climbers. Three hundred men showed up at the opening of his tent. He threw down the challenge. "I want you to climb the steepest, most severe unguarded face of this rock in the dead of night," he told them. He would give the first man to reach the top a handsome reward, in today's currency close to a half million dollars; a little less would go to the second man; a little less still to the third; and so on, until 12 men had reached the summit. Those who succeeded in reaching the summit after them would share in the glory of victory. All these men had to do was scale a giant, freezing, slippery rock in the dead of night with nothing but iron tent pegs, mallets, and ropes. This was extreme climbing at its most extreme. Yet all but ten of the 300 men made it to the top.

The climbers stationed themselves above the arrogant defenders of the rock. At the first light of dawn Alexander told his enemy to look up—he'd sent warriors with wings to conquer them. Oxyartes and his crew were so shaken they surrendered on the spot.

At the let's-kiss-and-make-up festival afterward, Alexander met—and eventually married—the chief's daughter, the beautiful young Roxane. Since Roxane came from an unimportant Afghani tribal clan, most historians figure that the marriage was truly made for love—or lust.

In 326 BCE, after securing all of Persia for his empire, Alexander decided that taking all of India sounded good too. He and his army crossed the Indus River, where the region's ruler, King Omphis, warmly welcomed them. But King Omphis had a bitter enemy deeper in the Punjab: King Porus. Alexander and Omphis created an alliance in order to take on Porus in what is today Pakistan. The Battle of the Hydaspes was Alexander's last major battle before his men began to mutiny and demand to go home. It was also the battle that nearly undid him.

It had been five years since Alexander's last major battle on an open field. Porus' army was smaller than Alexander's, but he had a secret weapon: elephants, 300 of them. Horses hate elephants, and the mere presence of them rendered Alexander's crack cavalry completely useless.

Once again, his enemy took a defensive position across a body of water, the Hydaspes of present-day Jhelum, and waited. The river was furious and swelling as the monsoons began to rage. The elephants unnerved Alexander's men and horses with their endless trumpeting. Nothing calmed his men, not even explaining that elephants were nothing but mice built to government specifications.

Alexander was stumped. He refused to attack under these circumstances, and Porus was in no rush. They would lie in wait, even as the rains came. It's at this point that Alexander displayed his genius for what Renault describes as "war psychology, cool nerve, swift reaction in an emergency, resource, organization, and leadership." Not to mention his ever-popular mind-fuck.

Day after day, he moved large formations of troops to different crossing points. He would launch boats and rafts, then pull them back. Porus' army kept scrambling into position, readying for the attack, only to witness a "just kidding" retreat. At night, Alexander marched his men to the edge of the river, where they blew trumpets and hollered war cries, forcing Porus to assemble his men and elephants to meet the phantom attack. Porus'

army—including his elephants—waited all night in attack position in the soaking rains. Alexander got a good night's sleep. Day and night—amidst the endless monsoon storms—Alexander pretended to attack. Porus was forced to respond every time. His army was tired, irritable, and confused.

But while Alexander faked attacks at different crossings on a continual basis, he also allowed Porus to see that he was building an outrageous store of food and supplies, implying that he was going to settle in to wait for the monsoons to end and attack in the fall. Porus was kept guessing at every turn. Alexander kept this up for two weeks. Meanwhile, his scouts had found a wooded area upstream that would block his crossing from view. While he continued the faux marching, trumpets, and war yells, he snuck his army across the monsoon-swollen river without Porus suspecting—all in one night. Modern military historians still shake their heads over that one.

Meanwhile, Alexander was consumed with trying to figure out how to use the elephants against their own handlers. It wasn't just the horses that were scared. His men were shaking in their sandals at the sight of them.

At the battle the next morning, Alexander took his cavalry to the far right, keeping his horses away from the elephant-heavy center, and his infantry went left. They had begun encircling the enemy. As the center swarmed with Porus' men and elephants, Alexander gave the order to his archers to first take out the elephant handlers (who rode on top of the beasts), then harass and injure the elephants. He didn't want the elephants killed. He wanted to cause an elephant stampede—stuck in the center, the only thing they could stomp on were Porus' own men. It was a brilliant strategy. Alexander had figured out how to use his enemy's own strength against him. In the ensuing chaos, Alexander's army soundly defeated Porus. It was to be his final masterpiece, though a sad one for him. His beloved horse Bucephalus died in the battle.

By the time he died in 323 BCE, when he was 32, Alexander

was the richest, most powerful man alive. He had subdued countless cities, tribes, and armies and defeated the king of the world's mightiest nation. He had taken possession of countless square miles of the planet, making him, centuries before Donald Trump, owner of the most prestigious addresses on earth.

Nobody before or since could claim to have won so many battles and taken over so much territory. By the time he was done he had conquered most of the known world (the Greeks weren't yet aware of a little hunk of land called China).

In a literal sense, Alexander became the first and only king of the world.

Chapter 7

The Bottom Falls Out

Hephaestion's death marked the beginning of the end of Alexander's life. Because he had patterned their 19-year relationship after the story of Achilles and his lover Patroklos, Alexander could not have felt optimistic: Achilles died only a short while after his lover.

Alexander was not in good health. He may have won every battle, but victory had come at a price—he had been wounded by every conceivable weapon, including a crossbow. The arrow had pierced his lung like a chicken satay. That he survived the arrow going in was a wonder; that he survived getting it pulled out is a miracle. He never fully recovered. Between his grief over Hephaestion's death, his growing reliance on alcohol, and a wound that made his body more susceptible to infection, his days were numbered.

Still, Alexander wasn't one to lie around feeling sorry for himself, even with his physically deteriorating body. He planned further campaigns along the Persian Gulf from his base in Babylon, about 30 miles south of modern Baghdad. Working out of the great palace of Nebuchadnezzar, Alexander got busy with grand projects. He didn't know any other kind. He set his sights on creating a permanent sea route to Egypt. But omens of his demise kept getting in the way. Deeply superstitious, Alexander and his men feared the worst.

One remarkable portent involved a crazy man who had wandered into Alexander's palace and sat on his throne (the one in the reception hall, not the bathroom). To the Greeks, seeing a stranger sit on the royal chair was the equivalent of having a black cat dart across your path as you walked under a ladder on Friday the 13th. When the man took Alexander's seat, the eunuchs wailed in horror but did nothing. The same custom that prohibited riffraff from sitting on the throne prevented eunuchs from removing anyone from it. The eunuchs called for the guards, and the man was dragged away. He was tortured to see if he was part of a plot, but he insisted he wasn't. But rather than being relieved that there wasn't a plot against Alexander, everyone became more nervous, for the event seemed an ever-darker portent of disaster.

The omens kept coming, working everybody's last nerve. Alexander sailed down the Euphrates to address the concerns of some Persian farmers downstream from Babylon. They couldn't get enough water from the Euphrates, which was ruining the petunias. "Not the petunias!" Alexander the Stewart exclaimed. He summoned a team of engineers to develop an irrigation system. While he was there, he settled a new town. The man was nothing if not productive. On his way back, Alexander took a brief tour of the Babylonian waterways and canals. He wore a Greek sun hat bearing the royal colors: purple and white. As the party sailed through the graves of dead Assyrian kings, the wind took Alexander's hat, which landed—wouldn't you know it—on top of a tomb.

You can imagine the hushed shock. One of the sailors fetched the hat and, in order to keep it dry, stuck it on his head as he swam back to the boat. Now, it goes without saying that you cannot wear the king's hat. His garters, maybe. But not his hat. The seers were shocked and saw it as another bad omen. First his ass, now his head. It seemed that one of Alexander's body parts was going to be handed to him on a platter. The royal guards beat the sailor badly, but Alexander rewarded him with money for his ingenuity.

This seemingly unimportant trip had another fateful twist to it. The waters they sailed carried sewage from the densely populated Babylon. Alexander got sick that very night during a huge feast of Dionysian proportions. (Did these people ever just snack?) Some say Alexander was poisoned. Some say his alcoholic ways caught up with him. He did, after all, buckle after draining the Cup of Heracles, which held six quarts of wine. Or,

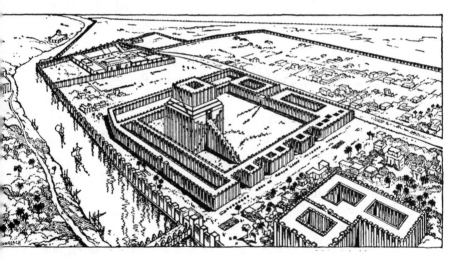

as historians increasingly believe, his food and water might have been contaminated by the aforementioned sewage.

In any case, Alexander left the feast and slept through the night and most of the next day. He started running a fever, but that didn't deter him from making plans for his next expedition. His condition got so bad he had to be carried around in a litter, a portable couch carried by hot, sweaty, handsome Greek guards. In fact, that's how Alexander came up with his drag name: Kitty Litter.

There is no record of an attending physician. If there were one, he probably would have been accused of murder. That was the tricky thing about being the king's doctor. It was an incredible honor, guaranteed to raise your status and standard of living—and, unfortunately, your odds of an untimely death.

Alexander's sickness advanced, as did his delirium. Then he developed pneumonia. Or was it typhoid? Or malaria? Historians still debate this. Whatever the case, Alexander's battle-ravaged body and weakened lung were giving out. He ordered his chief officers to his bedside. The junior officers stood outside the doors. Alexander was so weak he could not make himself heard. Everybody knew he was near death. He gave his royal ring to his general Perdiccas, but he could neither speak nor lift a quill to write his intentions, which left open the question of Alexander's successor.

Rank and file soldiers began to believe Alexander was dead and demanded to see him. Alexander had them march through his quarters, and he sat up as best he could to make eye contact with each man as he passed. No word on whether he forced the soldiers to march naked; the ensuing spike in his blood pressure would surely have been enough to abbreviate the scant time he had left.

Compared to his life, Alexander's death was relatively anticlimactic. He expired quietly from pneumonia or...whatever. But not before uttering a few theatrical words. When asked to whom the throne should pass when he died, he croaked, *Hoti to kratisto* ("To the strongest"). And then he went limp. A drama queen to the end.

Questions remain as to what he actually said. *Kratisto* and *Kratero* (Craterus) don't sound exactly alike, but a dying man with a rattling lung could surely mangle the sounds. Some say Perdiccas, who didn't like Craterus, conveniently misheard Alexander.

According to legend, Alexander didn't just expire. That would have been a letdown. Instead, here's what's said to have happened: Dark fog crawled across the sky, and a bolt of lightning cracked the heavens in two, releasing a giant bald eagle. The bronze statue of Ahura Mazda in Babylon quivered, then the eagle swooped down on a radiant star and slowly ascended to the heavens. As Renault describes it, "When the star disappeared in the sky, Alexander too had shut his eyes." Now that's more like it.

Alexander's wife Roxane got very practical after his death. She sent a royal message to Alexander's other wife, the Persian princess Stateira, summoning her to Babylon. Somehow, this royal message got there before the news of his death; otherwise the princess wouldn't have come. The pregnant princess arrived with her sister, Hephaestion's widow. Roxane had them both killed and ordered their bodies thrown in a well. Nobody was going to challenge her right to the throne through her son, Alexander IV. Roxane must have been channeling Olympias.

Unfortunately, Roxane met the same fate. Her son was put in jail at six and murdered, along with his mom, when he was 13. Nothing else is known about him.

Remember the Persian queen mother Sisygambis, who bowed to Hephaestion instead of Alexander when they first met her? She wasn't just Alexander's favorite fag hag; she also happened to be Stateira's mother. When Sisygambis heard of the deaths, she said goodbye to friends and family and killed herself by an ancient form of suicide: turning to a wall and refusing to eat.

Nearly everything about Alexander's burial is shrouded in

mystery. The only thing we know for sure is that the funeral procession, capped by a wheeled monument housing his body, started in Babylon. Where was it headed? Macedonia, the place of his birth and rise to power? The oasis of Siwah, where the oracle had confirmed Alexander's divinity? Las Vegas, where he was offered a 3,000-year deal with a percentage of the gross?

You'd think Macedonia or one of the other Greek city-states would have been the natural place for Alexander's resting place. Was he not their native son? Why would you bury one of the most important Greek warriors in non-Greek soil? The instability in Macedonia after Alexander's death made it impossible for him to be buried there. In fact, in just a few years all of Greece would slump like a mud hut in a monsoon. Besides, it was doubtful that Antigonus, Macedonia's new leader, would want Alexander's body back home, where everybody would continue to worship their demigod and compare Antigonus unfavorably to him. Better he should stay away.

Meanwhile, Ptolemy—Alexander's self-proclaimed half brother—grabbed Egypt like a carb addict going after a Krispy Kreme. On his way to pharaoh-hood, he stole Alexander's sacred remains and took them to Alexandria. This gave him the advantage of strengthening his legitimacy to the Egyptian throne. Plus, he would benefit from the prophecy of Alexander's favorite soothsayer. The seer had predicted that prosperity would come to the land where he was buried.

To this day, no one knows for sure where Alexander's tomb lies, whether it is intact or, most important, if the embalmer got the face right. It must have been a monumental building filled with untold riches, yet nothing is known of its whereabouts, though there is a general consensus that it's in Alexandria.

After Alexander died, all hell broke loose. Power struggles between his former generals resulted in murder, mayhem, and territorial partitions. When the dust settled, the claimants to the throne, collectively called the *diadochi* (Greek for "successors," Latin for "Does not play well with others"), murdered Alexander's only living relatives—his son, Alexander IV, and his mentally retarded half brother.

Watching from the afterworld (and, most likely, through Hephaestion's parted thighs), Alexander must have wept over the dissolution of his life's work. The unity he had created throughout his empire lasted as long as a paper dress on prom night. Virtually all of his officers renounced the Persian wives they had been forced to marry (in the king's hope of uniting their cultures). They'd had enough of Alexander's diversity bullshit and installed a pure "white" Macedonian rule in the territories they carved out for themselves. Alexander's empire split into four areas. Three of them were ruled by his generals. Asia Minor became independent. All the territories eventually fell to the world's next great empire: Rome.

Greece and Macedonia were ruled by Antigonus, one of Alexander's generals. He lost three wars against the Romans. By 168 BCE, Rome had an airplane lavatory sign stamped across all of Greece: "Occupied."

Alexander's most famous general, Ptolemy, ruled Egypt. It was the only territory the Greeks held on to for a period longer than the run of a hit TV series. The Ptolemaic reign in Egypt lasted for 300 years and produced the most famous of Egyptian queens: Cleopatra VII. Yes, *that* Cleopatra, the one portrayed by Elizabeth Taylor (when she managed to drag herself to the set after her all-night benders).

As great as the Ptolemaic rule was, the new breed still didn't follow Alexander's vision of respecting conquered cultures. Only Cleopatra, the very last Ptolemaic ruler (who also became a mistress to Julius Caesar), bothered to learn the native language.

Alas, Caesar wasn't interested in an equal partnership with the beautiful queen; he only wanted to siphon all of Egypt's riches to Rome. So Cleopatra turned to Caesar's top general, Mark Antony, and convinced him to mutiny against his boss in a desperate bid to keep Egypt free of Rome. She promised her new lover half her kingdom if he would lead her forces in defeating Caesar. When she heard Caesar had won, she knew the days of Egyptian autonomy were over. It was time to play kiss the snake. Cleopatra's death marked the end of Alexander's Hellenistic kingdom. The next period of history had begun: the Roman Empire.

Alexander became a mythical figure over time—a recurring character in folktales and epics worldwide. It's as if Alexander picked one last fight and yelled, "You want a piece of me?!" The world answered the way Hephaestion did over two thousand years ago: "Nai. Oh, Theos, nai!" ("Yes. Oh, God, yes!"). Everyone wanted—and took—a piece of Alexander. You'd think *Well, yes,*

of course the Greeks claimed him; but why would anyone else? After all, he was a foreigner who attacked them. He sacked their cities, enslaved many of their citizens, and sometimes burned their temples to the ground.

It's a testament to Alexander's complexity that some of the places he took over felt conquered while others felt liberated. Alexander was like a Rorschach test: He was whatever people read into him. If you hated monarchies and tyrants, he was a proto Hitler bent on world domination. If you loved diversity and tolerance, he was the first multiculturalist intent on establishing a tolerant world where rulers were respectful of racial and religious differences.

Reactions to Alexander also depended on how hard you fought him. If you fought hard, you lost big. If you didn't fight, you won big. Resistance meant death or enslavement, whereas acceptance meant religious freedom and economic growth. Alexander exercised a kind of paternalistic democracy. The more allegiance you pledged the more freedoms you gained.

Everybody came up with a story about Alexander, even the Jews. They pictured him kneeling before the Torah, overcome with the revelation of one universal God (rather than the multiple gods the Greeks worshipped). Meanwhile, Ethiopian legend has Alexander protecting the angel that holds up the world and tricking a giant dragon into swallowing a bomb.

It wasn't just the peoples he conquered who turned Alexander into a legend that lasted over 2,000 years. People from lands he never set foot on admired him too. From Iceland to China his name has been invoked as ancestor, patron, conqueror, and homo poster-boy.

There are as many views of Alexander as there were countries he conquered. He's remembered as a folk hero in Europe and western and central Asia, where they usually call him "Iskander."

Alexander's famous red silk banner is still displayed in parts of Turkistan and Afghanistan. In Iran they call him something we can't print here. He is remembered, rather correctly, as the destroyer of Iran's great ancient empire and as the man who leveled the holy city of Persepolis.

Even today many people claim they're descendants of Alexander, his family, or his soldiers. Some go as far as to say that their horses are descended of Bucephalus! In Greek that kind of claim is called, *alogo kopria* ("horse shit").

When he first died, sightings of Alexander were reported everywhere. People claimed they saw him hovering over potato fields, commanding a fleet of ships, or tending a flock of sheep. They were the ancient equivalent of Elvis sightings. Everybody claimed to have seen or known him. Legend has it that even mermaids believed Alexander was alive. Before sailing through a dangerous pass, sailors had to answer the mermaid's question: "How is the great Alexander?" If they wanted to pass safely, they had to answer, "He lives and reigns," although "He lives in Hephaestion's pants" would have gotten them through too.

Death was a great career move for Alexander. He got more offers than his agent knew what to do with. Though he was cautioned not to overexpose himself, he defied his management company, ICM Afterworld Ltd., and made appearances in the Koran, Chinese holy books, Icelandic folktales, and a few episodes of *The Love Boat*.

Thinking the Greeks beneath them—yet secretly sending their sons to Athens for the superior university education—the Romans initially took pleasure in excoriating Alexander. The republicans of Rome hated what Alexander stood for—a tyrannical monarchy they considered inferior to their own form of government. But by the time of emperor rule, Alexander was once again admired. Caesar wept when he compared himself to

Alexander. In fact, it was awestruck Roman generals who first dubbed him "the Great."

By the time of the Renaissance, eternal fame was assured for Alexander. He was a popular subject in works by master artists— the paparazzi of their day—who loved the epic qualities of his life. Sculptures and paintings of him abounded in fashionable halls, much like college kids hang posters of their pop heroes.

The world got its first look at Alexander on the printed page 500 hundred years after his death in a book titled *The Romance of Alexander.* It was translated from the original Greek into just about every language in the world, including Latin, Hebrew, Arabic, Syriac, Armenian, Persian, Coptic, Ethiopian, Spanish, Quenya, Esperanto, and Jive.

The book was an instant international success, the first literary blockbuster, so popular it stayed on *The New York Times* best-seller list for 800 years. It finally lost its slot to some German guy named Gutenberg, who invented the printing press so he could publish that other famous collection of romance, folktale, rumor, gossip, and fantasy: the Bible. In other words, the son of Zeus got his ass kicked off the best-seller list by the son of God.

Since few people could read, the gist of *The Romance of Alexander* was largely spread through oral tradition. Thus the story of Alexander proliferated throughout the world—even to the Far East, which Alexander didn't know existed.

Alexander's fate as the world's reigning international superstar was sealed when stories of his life were translated into Latin as Rome fell. Latin became the dominant language of the Western world, ensuring not only that Alexander's tale would always be told, but that his tail would always be kissed.

More than 2,300 years later, Alexander the Great still stirs up controversy. In the 1990s, Greece almost went to war when a piece of the former Yugoslavia, the Republic of Macedonia, broke away and wanted to use Alexander's star on its new flag. The two countries are still at each other's throats over the right to claim a man each considers its greatest native son.

Historians lick their chops at the thought of how the world would look today had Alexander lived to old age. It's entirely possible that the Crusades, the Inquisition, and the Holocaust wouldn't have happened if Alexander's love of and respect for different cultures had become a permanent part of the human psyche. Alas, we'll never know, unless another kick-ass homo arises to seize the stage of history from the straight boys (and closet cases) who tend to make such a bloody mess of things when they're in charge.

Chapter 8

A Makeover to Die For

The ancient world had crow's feet, sagging tits, and a loose box. Then Alexander gave it the kind of makeover that inspires Cher to dedicate songs to her plastic surgeons. Alexander didn't just inject a little botox; he radically transformed the face of the earth with a unique surgical tool called Hellenism, which spread Greek language, ideas, arts, politics, architecture, science, and philosophy to the rest of the known world. Don't confuse Hellenism with the equally important "Nellyism," which spread Greek musical theatre, flowing robes, Doric columns, rich Corinthian leather, and floral appliqués.

Alexander created the impossible: a world unified by one king, one language, one currency, and one hell of an experiment in religious tolerance and racial diversity.

Exporting his culture to every corner of the empire, Alexander franchised Greek thought the way McDonald's franchised American burgers. Every culture, race, religion, and society that has subsequently thrived in the region has been substantially shaped by Alexander's brand of Hellenism: Arabs and Asians, whites and blacks, Hindus and Christians, Islam and Judea.

No matter what religion you practice today, Alexander most likely exerted some influence on its development. No matter what gym you work out in, you can thank Alexander for perfecting the concept (though, admittedly, if there's one reason to hate the man, it's for making you feel guilty if you don't get off your fat ass and hit the elliptical trainer). If you're a scientist, architect, biologist, philosopher, writer, or artist, you've also been influenced by Alexander.

Aristotle encouraged Alexander to spread the brilliance of Greek thinking to the rest of the world. As a result of Aristotle's tutelage, Alexander looked at the whole world as a giant urban renewal project. Basically, he either gentrified dilapidated cities, burned them to the ground, or built them up from scratch. Alexander founded about 70 new cities in Turkey, Syria, Iran, Iraq, Afghanistan, Egypt, Lebanon, Libya, India, Pakistan, and Middle Earth. Next to Bill Gates, Alexander was the richest, most powerful man in the world. Imagine how his wealth and power would have grown if he had known how much oil was beneath his feet. Clearly, he would have had a shot at running Halliburton or the White House—or both (seems to be a package deal these days).

Greek became the official language of the upper crust, the business class, the government, the educated, and sometimes the great unwashed. As each new city or conquered territory was Alexanderized—er, Hellenized—it flourished with Greek philosophers, interpreters, stone masons, engineers, architects, playwrights, and personal trainers. In any one of these cities— from Egypt to India—a man could read the classics, stage a Greek play, sip wine under Corinthian columns, and add inches to his biceps with a money-back guarantee.

As we mentioned earlier, the word gymnasium finds its root in *gymnos*—nude—which is how the Greeks did their sit-ups, lifted their weights, and practiced their pickup lines. While every major city that came under Greek influence eventually had a gymnasium, the Greek affinity for nudity didn't go over well everywhere. After all, Persians were fashion-forward folks, what with their fuchsia silk jackets and striped balloon pantaloons. They were quite willing to bench press the weights, but the one thing they would not lift off themselves was the burden of fashion. Nudity was also problematic in Judea, but for different reasons. Jewish men wanted to blend in, but they couldn't—not when they were walking around with their caps off. No, not yarmulkes: foreskins. They were the only circumcised men in the health clubs.

Hellenism introduced the Greek party animal to the world's stuffed shirts. Alexander had lots of friends in the theater (no, really—he wasn't gay), and they could always be relied upon to perform a rousing Sophocles or Euripides play if the price was right (wine, wine, and more wine). Taking a cue from him, all the cities he left behind partied like it was 1999, and dance and drama festivals spread like wildfire.

It's hard to understate the impact of Hellenism. It was so persuasive that Sophocles was a hit in Persia, Euripides the rage in Afghanistan, the *Iliad* a triumph in India, and the *Odyssey* the toast of Asia Minor. It was not unusual for turbaned nomads to stand in line to watch Greek plays, although they nearly rioted when the got a look at Ticketmaster's ridiculous surcharges. In Armenia, archaelogists have dug up verses of Euripides that they think were used as school texts. When the Romans came knocking on India's door several hundred years after Alexander, they were shocked to find that the Indians already knew about the Greek gods (and preferred them to the Roman versions). Five hundred years after Alexander, Buddhist monks were still carving depictions of the Trojan horse along-side the image of Buddha. Even today, many of the statues of the Buddha show him wearing not a Nehru jacket, as you might suppose, but a tunic in the Greek fashion—a direct holdover from Hellenism. Hence, Buddha's greatest line about the nature of life: Chic happens.

With Hellenism came a renaissance of science and scholarship all over the Arab world. And Alexander's pet city—Alexandria in Egypt—was at the heart of it. The Library at Alexandria contained more than 40,000 scrolls and featured a scientific museum that attracted scholars from all over the world. And the best part? A state-of-the-art Imax theater showing the most controversial film of the time, *Alexander the Great: Greek God or Goddamned Greek?* The greatest library of the ancient world, the Library at Alexandria was burned hundreds of years after Alexander's death by fundamentalists who were enraged to find a copy of *Heather Has Two Mommies* on the shelves.

Although Athens was unarguably the center of the universe for philosophy—thanks to Plato's Academy, which continued to flourish for centuries—Alexandria quickly became the "it" place for intellectual and commercial pursuits. Huge advances were made in the studies of human anatomy, climatology, and electrolysis. Egypt's Alexandria became the epicenter of the financial and commercial world, with better agriculture, improved canals, a coin-based monetary system, and the first triple-X movie theater to show Jenna James doing anal. Hellenized astronomers in the East were so sophisticated they began—a full 1,500 years before Galileo—to challenge the view that the sun revolved around the earth. Alexander's expeditions also stimulated a tremendous amount of mapmaking. One mapmaker floated the heretical idea that the world was round and even gave a pretty good estimate of its circumference.

The Persian-Arab world flourished under Hellenism, but it all came to a crashing halt with the fall of Rome and the rise of Christianity, around 400 A.D. The West was plunged into economic chaos, religious intolerance, illiteracy, and disease. Trade routes shut down, isolating cities and sowing suspicion everywhere. Feudal societies reigned. Life was now about survival, not arête.

Christianity became hostile to everything that came before it. The first syllable in Hellenism pretty much summed up Christianity's view of it. So everything Greek went up the creek without a paddle. Greek works, traditions, and practices were banned, burned, and belittled. When Christianity came in the door, Hellenism went out the window. The world no longer had religious tolerance, racial diversity, economic prosperity, and artistic expression on its menu. Now, the only thing you could order was church on a bed of church with a side of church. Contact with the East diminished as the Christian world collapsed into itself, ushering in the Dark Ages. Hardly a trace of Greek life could be found in Europe for almost a thousand years.

Today, there is only one reason we know about Alexander and the enormous contribution he and other Greeks made to modern life: the Egyptians and Arabs. The Arabs, untouched by Christianity through most of the Dark Ages, translated Greek literary works into Arabic and preserved them. The irony is inescapable—we in the West know our heritage only because the people we conquered preserved it for us.

The West rediscovered its westness around 1095 C.E., when Christianity came a knockin' on Arab homes with a charming door-to-door landgrab and conversion effort called the Crusades. Christians thought Muslims defiled Jesus' birthplace by living in Jerusalem, and they wanted them out, never mind that they'd been living there for a thousand years.

For the next 200 years, Egypt and other Arab countries fought the Christians off, and the Crusades ended in stalemates. During and after the Crusades, trade routes opened up. It was in the 13th century that Arab translations of Greek works were "discovered" and translated back into Latin for the West. Greek traditions started out in Greek, got translated to Latin, were discovered in Arabic, got re-translated into Latin, and were ultimately rendered into English. Is that a clusterfuck or what?

When the West rediscovered the monumental beauty of Greek architecture—the brilliance of its philosophy and the ingenuity of its inventions—Italy, in particular, exploded with intellectual and artistic excitement, ushering in one of the most creative, prosperous, artistic epochs in history: the Renaissance.

The Arab world flourished under this new Hellenism, which introduced several heretical ideas—like education for the poor as well as the rich and for girls as well as boys. In some of the more progressive Hellenized cities in Persia and Egypt, children from all classes learned reading, writing, and arithmetic. And, like Alexander, they memorized portions of the *Iliad* and the *Odyssey.* They also learned "civilized" Greek behavior (presumably, this didn't include sacking your neighbor and taking all his gold).

The result of Alexander's Hellenism meant girls and women in ancient Afghan cities were better educated than their modern counterparts under fundamentalist Islamic rule today. Some ancient women during this period even became noted philosophers and poets. Others became recognized scholars and painters.

And as we mentioned before, Alexander was famous for respecting women (he had more fag hags than George Michael), and it made sense that this respect would filter down. In many of the cities he conquered, he forbade his men from raping the women, which had been a prerogative of victors in battle since time immemorial.

Alexander's genius lay in his understanding that commerce was the key to tying his empire together. How did he actualize that understanding? Through the expansion of major trade routes. His conquests broke down trade barriers between warring factions, stimulated economic activity, and encouraged the construction of new ports and cities. His plan was to make Babylon not only the hottest fictitious bar in *Queer As Folk,* but also the new financial heart of the Hellenized world.

The world's economies had boomed under Alexander. All of the gold won from King Darius the weenie put a massive amount of money into circulation, while his endless wars created a new demand for arms and iron. New roads were built to make transportation swifter, and since the business class in every culture spoke Greek, transactions became easier than getting Paris Hilton to strip in front of a camera. Most important, a uniform monetary system replaced the creaky system of exchange and barter, accelerating the rate of commerce to dizzying speeds.

For generations after Alexander, the new trade routes completely revitalized economic ties between East and West. And it made for some interesting mingling. For example, one philosopher—also a pupil of Aristotle—walked *3,000 miles* from Delphi to Afghanistan. He stopped at Hellenized cities and wrote pamphlets about the wisdom of the Jews ("Call your mother"), Persian magi ("Don't bellyache when you can belly dance"), and Indian Brahmins ("Don't have a sacred cow, man"). This was just the kind of thing that Alexander would have loved.

Alexander's religious tolerance was inspired by his own deep spirituality. Even as he sacked Persian cities, he showed respect to their priests, the magi, whom he brought into his inner circle. He would do the same with priests in Egypt and India.

Alexander did not believe in a master race or a superior religion. Nothing made this point more clearly than the pedigree of the oracle he sought to confirm his divine origin. He didn't go to a Greek oracle: He went to a Persian one, the oracle at Siwah. Alexander also dedicated himself to a hybrid version of the ruler of the gods—the Greek Zeus and the Egyptian Amon.

But it wasn't all incense and flowers. Alexander may have loved religion, but he was also a brilliant tactician. He saw what happened to cities when foreign tyrants removed priests and other religious leaders from power as the Persians did. The power base was always threatened with simmering hatreds, attempted murders, mutinies, rebellions, and plots against the state. He understood that it was easier to dominate countries that way only in the short run. By giving control back to the religious classes in many of the cities and kingdoms he conquered, Alexander earned their undying trust and loyalty, and, of course, their taxes.

This tolerance of and interest in other beliefs have endeared Alexander to many. Islam (yes, Islam!) names him as a prophet;

Jews have honored him in their writings; and many modern Hindu scholars believe that Alexander was the inspiration for Skanda, the god of war.

The only religion that really hated him was Zoroastrianism, whose Iranian followers called him "Iskander Gujaste" (Alexander the Accursed). In fact, they still call him that today. The Iranian Zoroastrians are the last surviving adherents of the ancient religion that Darius and his ilk followed. Alexander is reviled as the foreign devil who killed their priests and burned their sacred books. But it wasn't Alexander that decimated their numbers—remember, Alexander integrated their magi into his court. Rather, it was Islam—as it was spread by the Ottoman Empire hundreds of years later—that destroyed many of the "pagan" faiths, including Zoroastrianism.

Interestingly, Alexander is a hero to mainstream Islam because they believe he made the Arab world more receptive to the word of Allah. By creating a melting pot of Greek and Persian traditions, philosophies, and gods, Alexander unintentionally eliminated much of the pagan competition, which made the Arab world ripe for Islam.

In Persia, Alexander was often depicted in paintings and sculptures with curved rams horns springing from his lovely locks. Some historians think it's because Zeus-Amon was often portrayed with the horned head of a ram—like father, like son. Following this thread, most mainstream Muslim scholars believe that Alexander was the man behind "Dhul-Qarnain," the double-horned king named in the Koran. The ancient Muslim writings also state that Alexander built an iron wall to hold back the forces of chaos and destruction—a wall that will supposedly endure until Allah returns.

Islamic fundamentalists, however, foam at the mouth at the very thought that Mohammed thought well of a "Westerner."

It's rather inconvenient to claim the West is Islam's greatest threat when a Westerner created the circumstances that enabled Islam to flourish. So they claim "Dhul-Qarnain" refers

either to the Babylonian king Gilgamesh or the Persian king Cyrus II. Islamic fundamentalists are no doubt still angry that Arabs ended up spreading the Western way of life by translating Greek works into Arabic when Christianity had destroyed the last vestiges of it. If they'd had it their way, they would have joined their hated enemies—the Christians—in burning every bit of the Hellenistic legacy, including the works of Aristotle and Plato.

Before Alexander burst on the scene, religions tended to be local, tribal, or national. But after Alexander the world was one great big melting pot. Toss in Zeus and other Greek gods, add a pinch of Egyptian divinity, a smattering of Persian mysticism, a dollop of Brahman wisdom, and a sprinkling of Jewish lore. Then serve it up with a huge helping of oracle pie.

Interestingly, Alexander's Hellenism played a major role in shaping Jewish thought and in setting the stage for the success of a certain Jewish rabbi named Jesus. The Jews loved Alexander, primarily because he was one of the few conquerors who did not try to impose his own beliefs on them. That's quite a testament to the strength of Alexander's commitment to religious diversity. After all, the Jews believed in something Alexander must have considered insane: one god.

After the conquest of Tyre, Alexander visited Jerusalem, where the Hebrew archpriest met him at the gate. Instead of waiting for the priest to come to him—the typical royal protocol—Alexander jumped off his horse and walked toward the holy man.

This pissed off Alexander's general Parmenion. "The soldiers are angry that you rushed to greet him," he hissed. "The archpriest should have come to *you*!"

Alexander's response? "I did not greet the archpriest but the *god* he represents."

This stunning display of respect for other faiths was unprecedented in the ancient world. Actually, in any world. Is there any question that Alexander was way ahead of his time?

During his visit in Jerusalem Alexander asked that his statue be placed at Solomon's Temple. The archpriest resisted, saying that Jewish law forbids placing icons or statues in the temple. It must have been a scary thing to say no to the great Alexander, but the archpriest quickly offered an alternative. Every male child born that year to priests and their descendants would be named Alexander. His name—and legend, they promised—would live forever, which explains how such a goyish name ended up being common for Jewish boys. This compromise was enough for Alexander, and everybody breathed a sigh of relief. By the time he left, he had assured the Jews that they would be free to worship as they pleased (as long as they acknowledged him as their king and paid their taxes, of course). Some even say that the word *synagogue,* which is Greek, dates back to the command Alexander gave ensuring that the Jews could gather freely to worship.

But long after Alexander was gone, Hellenism became a huge problem for Jews. Hellenism was one big fat assimilation machine. You entered as a distinct member of a tribe and got burped out as a nondescript associate of a Greekified culture. Hellenism appealed to some Jews because they got to blend. Nobody likes to stand out in the crowd (you're an easier target for scapegoating that way). But from the moment the Jews claimed there was only one Guy in the Sky, they stood out, and there was nothing they could do about it.

Hellenization offered a respite. Jews could adopt Greek names and speak the language and nobody would know they were different (until they stripped at the gymnasium, of course). In their rush to appear "just like everybody else," many Jewish men opted for the world's first cosmetic surgery: foreskin replacement. It sounds like a joke, but, trust us, we're not that good.

As time went on Hellenized Jews began to assimilate so completely they no longer considered themselves Jewish. This didn't sit well with a minority of hard-core Jews who viewed assimilation as a threat to their survival. They staged a revolt against Alexander's Syrian successors, who were conducting a kind of "forced Hellenization" on Jews by demanding they pay homage to the Syrian versions of the Greek gods.

This band of scrappy Jews was known as the Maccabees. Their victory against the powerful Syrian army resulted in the creation of a new Jewish holiday: Chanukah. Today Chanukah is celebrated with the same prayer of remembrance as other Jewish holidays: "They tried to kill us. We survived. Let's eat!"

Interestingly, the Maccabees paved the way for Christianity 165 years later. After all, if the juggernaut of Hellenization had completely swallowed Judaism (as it had swallowed many different faiths, religions, and cults over time), there would have been no Jews. No Jews would've meant no Jesus. No Jesus would've meant no Christianity. And no Christianity would've meant no Mel Gibson exploiting the crucifixion of Christ for profit.

Beyond the vast influence of Hellenism, Alexander was the first to introduce the idea of multiculturalism. The irony is that Alexander's tutor Aristotle was a xenophobic racist pig. He thought non-Greeks were less than human. Alexander did not agree. Aristotle also advised Alexander to treat all Persians as servants and slaves. Alexander did not do so. Instead, he treated Egyptians, Persians, and Indians alike as kinsmen—at least the ones who acknowledged him as king. Those who didn't, he slaughtered, but, hey, nobody's perfect. By treating those people who acquiesced to him with dignity and respect, Alexander earned their loyalty. In turn, most of them treated him as a liberator and happily joined forces with him. This was political genius at its apogee. And utterly amazing for the times.

From the beginning, Alexander integrated his forces with local warriors—even as his Macedonian veterans howled in protest. They didn't want to fight alongside barbarians! They sneered at the outsiders, calling them Alexander's "ballet soldiers." But Alexander would not be deterred. He kept the peace within the ranks by placing the Macedonians in the front ranks carrying pikes, backed by Persians in rows behind them with swords and javelins. In other words, he put the Persians in the back of the bus. Still, this strategy was genius for the times. Alexander knew they'd be forced to trust each other in battle. Alexander also chose 30,000 Persian boys for military training. By teaching them Greek—and the Macedonian art of war—

Alexander was preparing the next wave of fighters and officers. This made the Macedonians jittery—and jealous—but Alexander was certain that a unified empire would only work with an integrated army.

As we saw earlier, Alexander also encouraged his officers to marry local women. Historians estimate that as many as 10,000 men took him up on it. Over the years, these unions resulted in thousands of children and large networks of extended families. It's a tribute to Alexander's hold over his men, most of them racists to the core, that they agreed to help Alexander achieve his utopian vision of an integrated world. In mid-twentieth century America most whites resisted desegregation and later fought forced busing of students between predominantly white and predominantly black schools. Imagine what their reaction would have been to forced miscegenation.

Alexander's thinking? It's hard to have an "us versus them" mentality when you're all sleeping in the same tent.

Alexander encouraged racially mixed unions by paying soldiers handsomely for marrying locals. He also promised to support their children. If the Macedonians decided they wanted to pack it in and go home, they were encouraged to leave their Persian families in Persia, under Alexander's protection. And they needed protection. The racism in Greece was intense, and Alexander knew that if the men traveled home with Persian wives and children, they would face tremendous hostility and discrimination. Alexander swore to his men that their families would be taken care of and that their children would be educated in the "Greek way" at state expense. He would personally hand over their sons to them when they had grown up. The brilliance of such a plan was that everybody was grateful to Alexander—the men who decided to go back home as well as the wives and children (who would serve under his command in the future) who stayed back.

Alexander's commitment to integration and unity is best exemplified by the mass wedding in the city of Susa (in present-day Iran) after the defeat of Darius and Bessus. There, Alexander married not one but two Persian princesses—one of them Darius' daughter—and officiated at the wedding of 92 Macedonian officers to Persian women. The celebrations lasted for five days. His idea was to create "a new ruling class of mixed blood, which would be free of all national allegiance or tradition."

Within months of the mass weddings, Alexander's officers were up to their ears with all his fancy talk about equality. They groused about the attention he "lavished" on his new Persian recruits. The officers wanted to go home, and they threatened to walk out on him. Alexander threw one of his famous bitch fits and shamed his men for doubting the son of Zeus. When his men finally begged his forgiveness, Alexander gave his "I Have a Dream" speech. "I regard you *all* as my kinsmen," he swore— meaning both Macedonians and Persians. According to legend, at the reconciliation banquet later at Opis, he made a famous prayer for harmony and fellowship where he is purported to have said: "I do not separate people, as do the narrow-minded, into Greeks and barbarians. I am not interested in the origin or race of citizens. I only distinguish them on the basis of their virtue. For me each good foreigner is a Greek and each bad Greek is worse than a barbarian."

Sadly, modern scholars can't find any proof that Alexander ever uttered those exact words. Most ascribe the Harmony Prayer to *The Romance of Alexander* or to medieval ballad writers. Still, the prayer seems consistent with his actions. And even if he hadn't put it in quite those words, there was no denying the profundity of his actions: Nobody had seen or heard anything like Alexander's appreciation of diversity in the ancient world.

Of course, no discussion of Alexander's legacy would be complete without addressing how he transformed the military. Not all of his innovation was necessarily good (especially for his victims), since it meant the adoption of war as an instrument of personal glory on a worldwide scale. Alexander's obsession with glory—glory that could only be obtained on the battlefield—meant that war had to be a constant affair. That's why he established a war hotline (operators greeted callers with, "Alexander the Great. How may we conquer you?"). No war meant no glory. And that was unthinkable to the Boy Wonder, who wanted to achieve more than Achilles and Heracles. His successors agreed with the idea that war equaled glory, so they stayed busy for decades—sometimes hundreds of years—pursuing wars and more wars.

Still, Alexander's military innovations were impressive. While it's true that Alexander inherited a world-class army from Philip, he single-handedly took it to new heights of excellence. The Macedonian army was the first professional army, the first army to pay its men, and the first army to demand allegiance under one king (unlike the small mercenary armies of old that fought under various rulers). The result was a national force that would serve as a model for all of history.

Philip and Alexander trained their army year-round, which was also a new concept. The phalanx, cavalry, light infantry, and siege corps honed their skills on a continual basis and also trained together in a coordinated effort. Nobody had ever thought to coordinate efforts before, and the innovation produced a fighting force that consistently decimated its enemies.

Alexander also created the *hypaspists,* a light infantry division (versus the heavy infantry of the phalanx) that could be used in lightning-quick maneuvers. These were the precursors of today's specialized units, like the Navy SEALs or the Harlem Globetrotters.

Alexander, a superb horseman, created the best cavalry unit in the world. So fast and powerful was his cavalry that he used it as his "shock unit." The cavalry would attack first, then quickly re-form as needed. Previously, the phalanx or heavy infantry was considered the "shock unit," but Alexander expanded his options to adapt to each new situation.

Finally, Alexander's most enduring military legacy is probably his leadership skill. No other military leader in history understood the psychology of leadership so well. For heaven's sake, how else do you get a vast army to follow you for a decade, covering 22,000 miles *on foot*? Julius Caesar, Cleopatra, Louis XIV, and Napoleon all wanted to know. They're just a few of history's elite leaders who studied Alexander's ways and tried to replicate them.

Alexander inspired extraordinary loyalty. He vowed never to ask something of his army he would not do himself. His ringing oratory was backed by decisive example. The man walked the talk. He was wounded by every weapon of war known at the time. He even jumped into the middle of an enemy citadel—*alone*—and fought until he was almost killed.

Alexander always honored fallen men with special funerals, often had bronze statues made of them, and ensured that their families were not taxed. He visited the wounded, clucked over their injuries, and listened to the men tell their individual stories. And he often did this while he himself was wounded. He would not leave anyone uncared for, especially if he was cute.

Alexander did not believe that his stature automatically earned respect from his men. First, there's no drama in that. Second, he believed in winning devotion by exemplifying the courage, bravery, and wisdom he expected of his men. If his men had to endure hardship, then, by God, he was going to show them how to endure it.

Alexander inspired bottomless loyalty by winning the hearts of his men—the ordinary army soldiers. He slept in a tent like them. He knew their names (thousands of them), honored their bravery, and was almost always the first to lead the charge.

Alexander the Great started out as a Teenage Mutant Ninja Turtle, turned into the Terminator, and died as Gandalf. History lurches forward and backward, but rarely as a consequence of the aspirations of a single man. Alexander was such a man. Calling him "the Great" does him an injustice. He is, in fact, Alexander the *Fabulous*, the man who brought the world to its knees.

Index

Index

Index

Index

Index